Francis of Assisi

Francis of Assisi

PERFORMING THE GOSPEL LIFE

Lawrence S. Cunningham

WILLIAM B. EERDMANS PUBLISHING COMPANY
GRAND RAPIDS, MICHIGAN / CAMBRIDGE, U.K.

Wm. B. Eerdmans Publishing Co.

255 Jefferson Ave. S.E., Grand Rapids, Michigan 49503 /

P.O. Box 163, Cambridge CB3 9PU U.K.

Printed in the United States of America

08 07 06 05 04   7 6 5 4 3 2 1

Library of Congress Cataloging-in-Publication Data

Cunningham, Lawrence.

Francis of Assisi: performing the Gospel life / Lawrence S. Cunningham.

p.   cm.

Includes index.

ISBN 0-8028-2762-4 (pbk.: alk. paper)

1. Francis, of Assisi, Saint, 1182-1226.

2. Christian saints — Italy — Biography.   I. Title.

BX4700.F6C7845   2004

271′.302 — dc22

[B]

2003064341

www.eerdmans.com

Contents

Francis of Assisi: A Modest Foreword   vi

1. Beginnings at Assisi   1

2. Francis and His Companions   30

3. Rome and Beyond Rome   48

4. Francis and the Rule(s) of the Lesser Brothers   65

5. The Stigmata of Saint Francis   79

6. Saint Francis and the Love of Creation   92

7. The Final Years   108

8. Francis Reconsidered   120

9. A Reading Essay   140

Appendix: The Prayer of Saint Francis   146

Index   150

Francis of Assisi: A Modest Foreword

A SPECIAL ISSUE of *Time* magazine in 1992 proposed a list of the ten most important personalities of the previous thousand years in anticipation of the celebration of the new millennium. In that distinguished list there were musicians (Mozart), inventors (Gutenberg), statesmen (Jefferson), explorers (Columbus), artists (Michelangelo), writers (Shakespeare), scientists (Galileo and Einstein), as well as two religious figures: Martin Luther and Saint Francis of Assisi. Such lists are a dime a dozen, showing up every time there is some momentous calendar event, and practically everyone would have amended *Time's* list in one way or another. What is curious, however, is the inclusion of Francis. What is it about this humble, semiliterate, medieval figure that should merit inclusion in such a litany of classic names?

This little meditative book will not attempt to answer the question just posed, although along the way it will give some indications that might help someone else to frame an answer. There are lines of inspiration rooted in the life and practices of Saint Francis that, in fact, had a shaping influence on the subsequent history of Christianity, an influence that spilled over into the larger shaping of Western culture.

In fact, this book will argue against at least one stereotype of the saint found in popular culture, mediocre Christian art, and even in some religious circles. It is a stereotype that can be traced back into the nineteenth century and, unlike most stereotypes, it is not even a half truth. It is, rather, the sentimentalizing of a very small truth. An earlier edition of the famous Butler's *Lives of the Saints* said, somewhat snippily, apropos of Francis in our own time, "that religious and social cranks of all sorts have appealed to him for justification, and he has completely won over the hearts of the sentimental." There is, in that observation made for Saint Francis on the day of his feast, October 4, more than a grain of truth. This book will work against that view of Francis that is most completely summed up by the ubiquity of those cast concrete garden statues of Francis with a bird perched on the saint's shoulder found at everyone's local garden center. Such an understanding of Saint Francis is coterminous with what I would call "spirituality lite."

That romantic view of Francis traces its ancestry back to the nineteenth century. The rediscovery of Francis as a precursor of the Italian Renaissance is as early as Frederic Ozanam's *Les Poetes Franciscans* (1849) and the occasional essays of Matthew Arnold. Paul Sabatier's *La vie de St. François d'Assise* (1893) triggered a century-long debate about whether Francis was a proto-evangelical. The Vatican honored that thesis by putting Sabatier's book on the index a year after its original publication. The Danish convert to Catholicism, Johannes Jørgensen, wrote a life of Francis that remained in print for decades after its publication in 1910. It was a direct challenge to Sabatier's understanding of Francis. In the twentieth century Nikos Kazantzakis's study of Francis turned the Umbrian saint into a medieval Zorba the Greek. Later in time Franco Zeferelli's saccharine film *Brother Sun, Sister Moon* (1973) made Francis into a hippy *avant la parole.* It is this Francis who has been the subject of any number of popular biographies, films, and even comic books published over the past two decades. One could multiply such instances of a romantic reading of Francis, but they are perhaps best understood as a tradition that has crystallized in those piously charming "blessings of the animals" so beloved of certain Episcopal rectors in this country.

Such a view of Francis is a shorthand way of thinking about the lamentable split that exists today between religion and spirituality. So often that split gets phrased in this fashion: "I am spiritual but not religious." The problem with "spiritual" as opposed to religion is that it can soon turn into self-centeredness, a lust for personal experience, and a kind of middle class therapy. Within that context, concrete statues of Saint Francis found in garden centers is "spirituality," but the Francis wounded by the marks of Christ on Mount La Verna is religion. It will be the burden of this book to argue that Francis of Assisi was the opposite of all of those specious "spiritual" characterizations; indeed, it could be said that he was, that his life was, a reaction against those very sentiments.

Without denying the clear charm of his persona, this work will attempt to put the life of Francis into the context of the reforming impulses of medieval Europe which sought to articulate the ideal gospel life (the *vita evangelica*). My study will look at Francis against that background in order to advance the claim that within that tradition, triggered by the cleansing reforms of Pope Gregory VII and his successors, he also was an original. Franciscan originality derived from the success that Francis had in "performing" the gospel. That performance, in turn, developed against the official attempts at church reformation which reached its zenith in the lifetime of Francis at the Lateran Council IV (1215). The impact of that reforming council is crystal clear in the writings of the saint himself. In other words, his life and message were a kind of existential exegesis of the scriptures in response to the reforming elements abroad in the church of his day. The success of his enterprise energized a flourishing new stream of "acting out" the gospel that not only affected religious thought and practice but also gave energy to those forces that, in fact, would give shape, among other things, to the Italian Renaissance. In other words, this little book intends to view the saint through the lens of theology.

It may also displease some people to learn that Francis was a devotedly orthodox Catholic with a keen sense of the juridical and sacramental life of the church, but that is an argument that I will also advance. Such an emphasis, to be sure, does not make Francis into a grim fanatic; after all, one of the words he loved to use was "joy" and his constant mantra was "peace." Neither of those words were uttered with naivete, although he did find joy where others might find disappointment and when he spoke of peace he did so against the grim violence so characteristic of his age. Nor does an insistence on his faith in the Catholic Church mean that he is closed off from other Christians and others who have admired him as a religious genius or that this book wants to hedge him in to some rigid fortress of narrow orthodoxy.

This book will conclude with some reflections on the modern rediscovery of the Franciscan charism in ways which range from a renewed reflection on theology of creation to the focus on the reality of the poor and service to them as a new way of conceptualizing theology. The lens through which this will be done is not unlike that of the earliest writers about Francis who saw him, his life, and his message as a source for deepening the Christian life.

This study would be for me a summary of my thinking about the saints as a resource for theological reflection in general and Francis as a model example for such an enterprise in particular. Early in my academic career I considered Francis in an anthology of texts published under the title *Brother Francis* (Harper, 1972); in a study of early Franciscan literature entitled *Saint Francis of Assisi* (Twayne, 1976); and a series of essays in a book of Franciscan art again titled *Saint Francis of Assisi* (Harper, 1981). Those works were, in a certain sense, immature; the writings of an enthusiast but an autodidact in Franciscan scholarship. I would like this work to be a more mature meditation on Francis, a kind of final word from my pen just as my other volume (*Thomas Merton and the Monastic Vision*, 1999) was a summary of my long engagement with that great contemporary figure. My basic stance will be to "read" Francis through my theological eyeglasses to attempt to reach up to his vision of how to lead the gospel life.

My justification for generally following the chronology of Francis's life is to provide context for the ways in which Francis understood the gospel against the background of his own experience within a quite distinct culture. A chronological approach is also useful in noting the many conversions of Francis as his life played out. In using a chronological framework, this book stands within the tradition of Franciscan biography, which is a never-ending stream. The classic, as many have reminded us, has a "surplus of meaning" so I feel no compunction in going over paths others have already trod. Indeed, while working on this book several popular biographies of the saint have been published, but none have exhausted the significance of the saint; indeed, most have that patina of romanticism that this book tends to downplay.

Studying Francis has become easier now that we have the multi-volume set of early documents (*Francis of Assisi: Early Documents* [New City, 1999-2001]) ably translated and edited under the general editorship of three Franciscan friars. In my citations of this early literature I use their work unless otherwise noted. Since the abbreviations of the writings of the saint and those of his commentators has not been standardized I will simply cite the traditional titles of these early works, identifying the titles in question in the text itself. Nor will this text employ footnotes, but a final chapter will provide an excursus on Franciscan scholarship or, better, a portion of the vast landscape of that scholarship that I have managed to embrace.

This book offers nothing new or radical in its meditation on the saint. That Saint Francis was a "classic" is accepted by everyone, but his classic status as a resource for theological reflection has been largely limited to those authors who speak within and to the Franciscan order. My aim is to enlarge that river of theological and spiritual reflection for a larger audience. In other words, this book merely hopes to capture some of that overflow.

*   *   *

These pages were written in such leisure as I found while carrying on my duties as a member of the department of theology at the University of Notre Dame. My congenial colleagues and the staff of the department of theology create an environment in which it is possible to find some leisure for writing. I would like to thank, in a particular way, Professor John Cavadini who makes life so agreeable in the department, and my wife Cecilia who makes it such a pleasure to come home each evening. My two daughters, Sarah and Julia, study under the shadow of the Golden Dome and are constant close reminders of all of the wonderful students here at Notre Dame who inspire us in ways they themselves do not recognize. On more than one occasion I have said to friends that some students in my class make me feel as if I am not worthy to teach them.

I would like to dedicate this book to the memory of the Franciscan Sisters of Allegany, who were my teachers from grammar school through high school at Saint Paul's parish in St. Petersburg, Florida. They were the first who taught me to love the Little Poor Man of Assisi. It is a very small token of respect for all of the religious women who made the American Catholic Church what it is today.

LAWRENCE S. CUNNINGHAM
The University of Notre Dame

CHAPTER ONE

Beginnings at Assisi

. . . fertile costa d'alto monte pende

Paradiso 11:45

THE UMBRIAN BIRTHPLACE of Francis, the town of Assisi, rests on the eastern flank of Monte Subasio. The town is situated about one hundred miles northeast of Rome and almost an equal distance south of Florence. Today's visitors almost unanimously praise its beauty because of how much of the medieval town seems intact and because of the pinkish hue of the stone, hewn from the local quarries in and around Mount Subasio that broods over the city. Despite the tour buses and the inevitable souvenir shops there is something, well, quite Franciscan about the place. It was not accidental that the great interreligious prayer service at which Pope John Paul II participated in 1986 was held in Assisi. Pilgrims and visitors of every religious persuasion see this lovely Umbrian town and the saint who has made it famous as their own.

Assisi is a place with a long history. The Etruscans had settled the area long before the advent of Christ, as later did the

Umbri from whom the area gets its name, and later still the Romans. The most distinguished resident of the city before Saint Francis was the Roman poet Sextus Propertius, born fifty years before the birth of Christ and dying circa 16 B.C.E., who occasionally hymned the beauty of the area in his poetry, although he was best known for the passionate love poetry addressed to his mistress, a poetry erotic enough to bear comparison with Catullus. Centuries later Francis, of course, would also praise a woman he loved — Lady Poverty — but with a quite different vocabulary.

Assisi has its fair share of Roman remains visible to this day, but none more conspicuous than the little temple of Minerva, now a church dedicated to the Virgin Mary, that sits in the center of the town's main square. The temple was famous enough to merit a side trip in 1786 by Goethe who, on his way south, stopped to admire the wonderful lines of the temple while showing at the same time absolutely no interest in either Francis or the art inspired by him that adorns the basilica where the saint's body rests. In fact, from his carriage, Goethe glanced at the basilica of St. Francis on his way to the town square and pronounced it a Babylonian pile. He then hurried on to Perugia, the ancient enemy of Assisi. Goethe's attitude was common enough in the eighteenth century.

When Francis was born in 1181 (or, by some reckonings, 1182) there were four architectural monuments that symbolized, each in its own right, the highly stratified social tensions in the town. High above the city was the fierce-looking citadel known as La Rocca Maggiore, the traditional seat of power of the old feudal aristocracy which, at the time Francis was born, housed a German agent of the Holy Roman Emperor. In the town itself the old cathedral *(duomo)* dedicated to the Virgin was the church of the powerful aristocratic bishop who held, in the name of the church, about half the lands in the area. Curiously enough, Assisi had a second cathedral, dedicated to its fourth-century martyred saint, San Rufino, built with the aid of the new class of rich mercantile interests who competed in prestige and power with the older feudal lords and the bishop who represented aristocratic interests. Between the canons of San Rufino and the bishop there were strained relations. The fourth center of power emerged during the lifetime of Francis: the city hall *(palazzo del commune)* that represented the growing secular and political power of the urban rich and a sign of the growing sense of civil life in medieval Italy. Below the "centers of power" represented by these architectural monuments was, of course, the roiling sea of beggars, day laborers, craftsmen, local traders, farmers, and herdsmen who made up what Francis was to call the *minores,* the little ones who stood economically and politically beneath the *majores* who endowed the cathedrals of the day and negotiated their business in the city hall.

That pinkish hue to the stones quarried from the mountain which so enchants visitors today masks the violence that was part of life in Francis's own time — violence of vendettas, street brawls, warring families, grotesque forms of public torture or execution, and class struggles. The grandees of the city would build towers at their homes not only to show power but also as fortresses to protect them when the inevitable vendettas would break out. It is against that aura of urban violence that we must understand the Franciscan cry of "Peace!"

It was into this complex but relatively small world, slowly

evolving from a feudal to a mercantile culture, that Francis was born. Like all Assisians of his class he was baptized shortly after his birth, with the name "John," at the cathedral font. His mother's name was Pica (other sources say Giovanna) and his father, Pietro da Bernadone. Although his baptismal name was John, his father renamed him Francesco (the "little Frenchman"), most likely as a tribute to France where Pietro frequently visited in pursuit of his business in the cloth trade. It was not a common name at the time.

Some scholars have tendered the suggestion that the family may have been Jewish by ancestry, a theory resting largely on the slender thread of evidence that the early biographer Thomas of Celano seems to deprecate the Christian roots of the family and because Pietro was in the cloth trade and a reputed moneylender — common occupations of the Jews of the time. There is no consensus on this point, which is very much a minority opinion, asserted but hardly proved.

Francis was born into the reasonably well-off mercantile class who identified their fortunes with the city hall and with the newer cathedral of San Rufino, although Francis probably was baptized in the old cathedral since San Rufino was not quite complete when he was born. This merchant group would find itself at loggerheads with the old feudal aristocracy. Most likely, his father applauded the siege of the fortress of La Rocca, when Francis was barely in his late teen years, with the resulting expulsion of the feudal lords resident there and the destruction of their fortified towers and castles, and it is equally probable that he contributed to the forces that did the deed. That siege, in 1198 and 1199, saw the expulsion of Duke Conrad of Urslingen and his followers with the result that Assisi now came under the political patronage of Pope Innocent III.

Interestingly enough, among the nobles who fled Assisi was the Offreduccio family of the future Saint Clare. It is clear that Francis grew to maturity at a time when his kind of family was very much in the ascendent and very much antagonistic to the aristocrats with their prideful sense of nobility and their unearned wealth. Within a few years, however, the aristocrats would return and the merchants would have to help rebuild the noble towers and palazzi, which explains how Clare got back to Assisi from her place of exile in Perugia.

Francis was raised in relative wealth. His education was, as far as we can tell, meager and local. Years later Francis himself, in his *Testament,* describes himself as unlettered *(idiota),* which means only that he had precious little formal education. That he could write we know because we possess a few autographs. That he knew some French (Learned from his father? On travels with his father to France for market reasons? As part of the musical culture of the time?) is stated in some of the early recollections of Francis that have him singing in that language. There are charming portraits of him later in life walking through the woods, pretending to play a violin with two sticks he picked up, singing in French.

Most of his education came probably at the hands of the priests of his parish church of San Giorgio where he learned some Latin, most likely using a psalter as a textbook, and some skill in writing. Writings from his own hand show little Ciceronian polish. He probably picked up some commercial skills in computation from working in the cloth trade with his father. There is no evidence that he yearned to go to Bologna for the university that was then the place for upwardly mobile young Italian men to attend because of its famous law faculty. His world was the practical and local world of business.

One thing all the early legends agree on is that in his youth he was far from a model of piety or virtuous living. His earliest biographer, Thomas of Celano, in his first life of the saint says bluntly that he wasted his life from the time of his childhood until he was twenty-five, charging him, specifically, with a love of frivolity, a penchant for extravagant clothing, and for being a "squanderer of his property." Interestingly enough, Thomas blames this dissolute style of life on Francis's parents who "reared him to arrogance in accord with the vanity of the age." Thus, Thomas concludes, "by long imitating their worthless life and character he himself was made more vain and arrogant." In his second life of Francis, Thomas would have him as a glutton and street brawler. Later biographers would add further salacious details to this catalog: he loved lewd songs, pranks, mindless vandalism, and so on. Only Saint Bonaventure, writing an "authorized" life much later in the thirteenth century, softens the image of a wild youth by emphasizing his innate generosity and moments of Christian passion. In the process, the negative picture of his own family also gets softened.

Not to put too fine a point on it: Francis seems to have been a typical indulged, wealthy, spoiled, and thrill-seeking adolescent who was indulged by a family who could afford to look with a benevolent eye on the peccadilloes of youth. What the early biographers describe, with the paradigmatic example of Augustine's *Confessions* in the back of their mind, was the portrait of a young man whose life was spent without aim or purpose but supported by a family who could afford to underwrite his whims. Francis seems to have done all the things that adults deplore in the youth of today: waste time and money; be preoccupied with fancy clothes which had to be in the latest mode; run around with the wrong crowd; chase after women; and take an interest in subversive music — in his case, the love songs *(chansons)* introduced from France.

When he was in his late adolescence Francis seems to have begun to grow out of this feckless life. The early authors do not seem very precise about how this change in his life came about. Some mention an extended period of illness. In a brief war in the fall of 1202 between Assisi and its traditional enemy from Etruscan times, the city of Perugia, Francis evidently went to war with his fellow bravos but ended up captured and held in the prison of Perugia's city hall. More than likely Francis, as a child of wealth, proved a fine bargaining chip in a ransom negotiation. After nearly a year, his father ransomed Francis, who was by then ill.

It goes without saying that periods of enforced recuperation from illness or times of enforced isolation figure large in the slow conversion of some people. Centuries later, healing from a battle wound was instrumental in the conversion of Ignatius of Loyola, and one could fill a small library with books written by persons who were imprisoned for a long period of time who use their silence and solitude to map a new way of life. Such books include Boethius's *Consolations of Philosophy,* written in Pavia in the late Roman period; the extraordinary letters written by Dietrich Bonhoeffer, who languished in a Nazi prison; and the prison writings of the Italian thinker Antonio Gramsci who suffered from the enforced hospitality of the Fascist government of Italy.

All of the early authors agree that, after his rescue and recuperation from whatever illness he suffered, Francis decided to take up arms as a knight. Along with a friend he left his family home in Assisi bound for Apulia in the south of Italy, where he intended to put himself under arms with a lord named Walter of Brienne who was raising an army as part of the militia of Pope Innocent III. After only a day's journey to Spoleto, however, something happened that caused Francis to return to Assisi a changed man. What happened has never been clear, but whatever it was it deterred him from going off for military fame. It may well be that he heard of the death of Walter of Brienne while he was traveling south to Apulia. The records do not show any "road to Damascus" conversion drama, but he clearly repented of his plan for military glory. His biographers, naturally enough, read this incident as a kind of premonition, which they tout as prophetic dreams of victory that would change him into a new, spiritual kind of warrior.

However much Francis may have turned his back on the chivalric ideal, he did not fail to learn powerful lessons that came from the romance tradition that praised it. More than one scholar has noted that the chivalric ideal held in high esteem two important virtues. The first was liberality *(largesse)* by which the knight gave freely and abundantly of himself and his goods. The second was courtesy *(cortesia),* a favorite word of Francis. By courtesy he did not mean manners but a certain gentle way of relating to the other. Saint Thomas Aquinas would later discuss this virtue of courtesy using the Latin word *affabilitas,* weakly translated into English as "affability." The word *cortesia* shows up frequently in the mouth of Francis — most famously, perhaps, when later in his life his eyes were to be cauterized with white hot irons. He looked at the physician's instrument and said, "Brother Fire, I pray you, be courteous to me." It is the rare poet, G. K. Chesterton once remarked, who remembers his poetry in a moment of dire danger.

Francis himself, in a rare moment of autobiographical testimony, treats his change in his life in a much more abbreviated fashion. In the beginning of his *Testament,* written a few years before his own death, Francis opens with these laconic words:

> . . . for when I was in sin, it seemed too bitter for me to see lepers. And the Lord himself led me among them and I showed mercy to them. And when I left them, what had seemed bitter to me was turned into sweetness of soul and body. And afterwards, I delayed a little and left the world.

While the early writers attribute a number of steps by which Francis left the world to become a man of penance, the saint himself singles out his changed attitude toward lepers. There is a reported incident in the early legends that he met a leper while out riding his horse and gave the leper some alms out of a sense of pity. It might have been that moment that Francis recalled, but we are not absolutely certain.

Medieval law stipulated numerous draconian rules to isolate lepers from common society even though the term "leprosy" most likely covered any number of disfiguring diseases like elephantiasis or the visible ravages of tertiary syphilis. The afflicted had to wear gloves and keep a clapper to sound when people came near. They lived in separate camps outside city walls. They could not speak to children or use any still (well) water for drinking or washing. An early statute in Assisi forbade any leper from walking in the town. Those that did so could be struck by everyone "with impunity." A quasi-funeral mass in honor of Lazarus (see Lk 16:20) was celebrated in some places as part of their ritual separation from society. Canon #23 of the Third Lateran Council (1179) insists that the lepers should have their own churches, access to the sacraments, and cemeteries for their dead. In the Assisi of Francis's day there were about five dwellings of lepers outside the town. Lepers, in short, were highly segregated in fact and feared as a matter of custom. Their very continued existence depended on the charity of people of good will since they could have no intercourse with regular society.

Despite the dread of leprosy there was a deeply embedded concern for lepers — a concern developed from stipulations found in the New Testament. Jesus had compassion on them, touched them, and cured them. It is worth noting that when Jesus heals the leper the evangelists quite explicitly note that Jesus reaches out his hand and touches the leper (Mt 8:2; Mk 1:41). Disregarding the law of purity whereby such contact rendered him ritually unclean, Jesus made explicit and open his contact with the leper by the gesture of touch. He did not keep the prescribed distance demanded by the custom and law of the day. The interaction of Jesus and lepers must be read against the purity codes of Leviticus where the leper is at least as polluted as a polluted house and more like a person with abnormal bodily discharges (see Lev 15:2-12). The Christian spiritual tradition was not slow to note the willingness of Jesus to touch a leper. It became, as it were, a test for anyone who aspired to take on Christ as model and exemplar.

In the hagiographical tradition great saints ministered to them. Compassion for the leper was held up as a heroic act of love. Furthermore, the tradition saw a nexus between Christ himself and the leper. The Vulgate translation of the Bible, glossing Isaiah's description of the Suffering Servant, sees Jesus, in Jerome's words, as *quasi leprosus* — like a leper. The subsequent tradition of Christian art would sometimes depict Christ as suffering leprosy, as the French iconographical motif of *le Christ Lepreux* testifies. The apex of that theme, of course, is depicted in the overpowering crucifix painted by Matthias Grünewald for the Isenheim altarpiece at Colmar at the end of the fifteenth century, which was situated in a hospice for sufferers of skin maladies. There was, in short, a powerful ambivalence in place vis-à-vis the lepers: they were to be shunned because of the (largely mistaken) fear of instant contagion but they were also an opportunity for the Christian to exercise the most compassionate form of charity by aiding them and sympathizing with their plight. Lepers invoked, in short, a combination of horror and compassion. In any case, the lepers were a direct challenge to those who took the gospel seriously.

Why does Francis, looking back on his youth, single out his conversion to the lepers as the nodal point in his life? He does not tell us beyond the affirmation that God led him to them; he did not go to them out of any natural sympathy. One can assay, however, some reasons for this turn to the leper. First, the lepers were the most ostracized persons in medieval society. To succor them was, in a real sense, to identify, albeit fleetingly, with those who were on the opposite pole of the important people — the *majores*. Francis was increasingly becoming a countercultural person. He gave up the life of the knight; he was, as we shall see, increasingly indifferent to family wealth and public prestige. Later in his life, Francis would still hold care of the lepers as a natural occupation for his lesser brothers, as the early friars were called. In the 1221 draft of his rule of life he assumed his friars would work with lepers, but he did not want them dealing with monies for them unless, as he writes, there was a "manifest need" (Rule of 1221). In its earliest phase, the Franciscan movement seems to have considered service to the lepers as a natural part of their novitiate. The charming compendium of vernacular stories known as the *Fioretti* includes an entire chapter on Francis's continuing love for lepers. The author notes that "not only did Francis willingly serve the leper but he also ordered the brothers of his order to serve them for the love of the Lord. . . ." That order gets spelled out in more precise detail in the *Mirror of Perfection,* which recalls that Francis said that when one enters their order "noble or not . . . it was necessary that they serve the lepers and live in their houses."

More important than the fact that Francis served the lepers was his gospel insight for doing so: in working with lepers he was doing so in imitation of Christ who received the lepers. In that sense, Francis "performed" the gospel that was the inspiration of his life. The equation was simple enough: If Christ served the abandoned lepers so should his followers. He would have been familiar with the common theme in the lives of the saints (for example, Saint Martin of Tours) that those who serve the poor and outcast often find, by dream or revelation, that they are serving Christ. That popular belief was a "filling out" of the words of Jesus recorded in Matthew 25 that when one aided the "least of the brethren" one did it to Christ. There was no group who more qualified as the "least of the brethren" than the lepers of the day. Assisi afforded Francis a perfect opportunity to carry out this command since its environs contained two rather large leper colonies — one dedicated to Saint Mary Magdalene and the other under the patronage of San Salvatore, the Savior — as well as at least three others within walking distance of the town.

If Francis found compassion for the leper to be the axial moment of his conversion, the early biographers also put much emphasis on another change in Francis that would soon bring him into confrontation with his father. Francis took some of his father's stores of cloth and sold them in order to have money for alms and to rebuild the broken down church of San Damiano. While praying before a crucifix, Francis heard instructions coming to him from Christ to "rebuild my church." Such a crucifix would have been done in the Italo-Byzantine style common in the period and which is still seen in Assisi to this day. Those crucifixes were not sculpted figures attached to a cross but monumental wooden panels on which the figure of the crucified Christ was painted.

The significance of Francis hearing the words of Jesus from the cross early in his career should not be overlooked. It formed the first part of a parenthesis that came to its conclusion decades later when, on Mount La Verna in 1224, he had a vision of a crucified man enclosed within the wings of a seraph. Anyone tempted to sentimentalize the saint needs to recall that his life from his youth to his final years forms a great *inclusio* bracketed by the Crucified One.

Francis took these words from the cross quite literally. He set out to gather material and actually began working at the reconstruction himself — an unthinkable act for a member of the gentry. Persons of his class simply did not work with their hands. Francis's bizarre behavior irritated his father greatly. If he was tolerant of Francis the young gallant-about-town, he saw the family honor shamed by Francis's increasing attention to the poor and by his work on San Damiano and other semi-ruined churches in the area. This odd behavior was all the more intolerable since Francis was doing it with Pietro's hard-earned money, and Pietro was nothing if not a hardheaded businessman who knew the value of a coin earned in commerce. The father first responded to these excesses by clapping Francis in his cellar until he came to his senses, but this strategy came to naught with the maternal intervention of Pica who set her son free.

The antagonism between father and son came to a head in one of the more famous scenes in the life of Francis. His father brought Francis before Guido, the bishop of Assisi, with the dual purpose of knocking some sense into the head of Francis and of recovering his lost money. The early chroniclers intimate that it was not so much family reconciliation but the return of his funds that the father most desired. That may or may not have been the case; the early Franciscan disdain for money might have figured in this interpretation of the struggle. At any rate, the encounter before the bishop now brought the private family rift between son and father into the public arena.

We have two famous visual descriptions of this father-son encounter. One is a fresco in the upper church of the basilica of Saint Francis in Assisi once attributed to Giotto but now more plausibly attributed to an unknown painter called the Master of the Saint Francis Cycle, even though some scholars still see the hand of Giotto in some of the works. The other depiction is a fresco certainly by Giotto done in the Bardi chapel of the Franciscan church of Santa Croce in Florence executed sometime in the 1320s. Both paintings take their inspiration from the description of the event found in Saint Bonaventure's *Legenda Major* since the other, earlier, *legenda* had been suppressed in favor of Bonaventure's account and were not easily available after the middle of the thirteenth century.

In the upper church of San Francisco in Assisi, the artist sets his scene in the main square of Assisi. Even the architecture in the background divides the two groups. To the left is the figure of Pietro Bernadone and his entourage and to the viewer's right is the nude Francis, covered by the cope of Bishop Guido with the sympathizers of Francis forming a cluster around the bishop. We should not overlook the symbolic importance of Bishop Guido who, after all, belonged to the propertied class. That he should mediate between Pietro (with whom he would have a natural affinity) and Francis is striking. Pietro holds in his arms the clothes of Francis and the other materials which he had taken from his father's storehouse. The fresco by Giotto in Florence makes a similar division into parties, but the architectural background is not in sharp contrast.

From a purely symbolic point of view one could not find a more explicit theological statement than what one finds in these famous depictions. There is a clear division between the world of the merchant and the world of the penitent Francis. The cloaking of the young man with the bishop's cope reads as a clear statement of Francis exchanging his natural paternity for the maternal embrace of the church. The artistic space between Francis and his father only hints at the chasm between

St. Francis renouncing all his worldly possessions
The Master of St. Francis Cycle, Upper Church, Assisi

Erich Lessing/Art Resource, NY

Another rendering of St. Francis renouncing all his worldly possessions
Giotto, Bardi Chapel, Florence

the natural and heavenly father. There is, in these scenes, a clear and explicit message about two of the oldest tropes in Christian ascetical spirituality: flight from the world *(fuga mundi)* and contempt for the world *(contemptus mundi)*. To choose this new path of life demanded explicitly to abandon the old.

One should not underestimate the symbolic power inherent in Francis's rejection. Pietro represented the rising new reality of late twelfth-century life: the rise of the money-earning entrepreneur whose skill in the making of money had given power to a new class of people. In early times it was the possession of physical power that counted; now it was the possession of wealth. As Adrian House, a recent biographer of Francis, has noted, Francis's emphasis on poverty and non-possession was a prophetic rejection of the nascent capitalism of the late twelfth century symbolized by the success of his own father.

In this dramatic separation of father and son there is another fundamental theme in Franciscan literature that is only hinted at in the twin depictions by the Master of the Saint Francis Cycle and that of Giotto: the theme of nudity. Francis stands enveloped within the protective cope of the bishop because he had stripped himself completely of his clothes; Bonaventure's *Legenda Major* makes a point of noting that Francis took off even his underclothes.

At one level this dramatic stripping off of his clothes represents a working out of a favorite metaphor of Saint Paul who uses such an image to distinguish the old life of sin and the new life in Christ: "Do not lie to one another, seeing that you have stripped off the old self . . . and have clothed yourselves with the new self" (Col 3:9-10); or, more pertinently: "You were taught to put away your former way of life, your old self, corrupt and debased by lusts, and to be renewed in the spirit of your minds, and to clothe yourselves with the new self, created according to the likeness of God . . ." (Eph 4:22-24). Perhaps, also, there is an allusion to the trope of "putting on the armor of God," harkening back to Francis's turning away from the warrior life when he first began his life of conversion. That Pauline image (Eph 6:11ff.) carries with it the twin movements of despoiling and rearming — but rearming not with the secular instruments of war but the clothing of spiritual combat or, as Saint Paul, phrases it, "cast off the works of darkness and put on the armor of light" (Rom 13:12).

The symbolism of putting off the old and putting on the new, taken from scripture, stands behind the ancient monastic custom of leaving aside secular clothes and adopting the monastic habit. In Thomas of Celano's *First Life* he alludes to that highly symbolic gesture when in his opening chapter he introduces his discussion of Francis's unconverted life with the heading "How he lived in the Clothing and Spirit of the world." Clothes, of course, had and continue to have a decided social signification. It was often legislated, for example, what kind of clothes a prostitute was to wear. What one wore or dared to wear was a preoccupation in medieval and renaissance society. Sumptuary laws designed to limit outrageous fashion were a commonplace, and fine clothing carried with it a certain sense of decadence and self-indulgence — a sense that has roots in the New Testament itself. Jesus, in praise of the ascetic John the Baptist, siezes on the clothing metaphor almost naturally: "What then did you go out to see? Someone dressed in soft robes? Look, those who are dressed in soft robes are in royal palaces" (Mt 11:8). It is remarkable how often Francis or his biographers remark on clothing and its symbolism — a frequency that we shall note in appropriate places.

Another important theme emerges in the early Franciscan chroniclers when they note that by stripping himself of his secular garb Francis is standing naked in the public square in Assisi. The classic formulation of an old spiritual dictum spoke of "nakedly following the naked Christ" *(nudus nudum Christum sequi).* That saying goes back at least to the time of Saint Jerome who uses it, in almost those exact words, in one of his letters. The Fathers loved to play with the concept of the naked Christ: born without clothing in his nativity and stripped by the Roman soldiers before his crucifixion. To crucify a person naked was to bring that person to further shame by exposing the person to the gaze of the crowd.

The Christian spiritual tradition saw in the nakedness of Jesus as an infant an indication of his true humanity as well as a recapitulation of the nakedness of the first Adam who, in Edenic innocence, was naked and without shame. The about-to-be-crucified Christ was left naked by the Roman executioners to shame him. The spiritual tradition was almost unanimous in seeing that humiliating gesture of the Roman soldiers in the light of Saint Paul's classic passage that speaks of the self-emptying of Jesus (kenosis): "though he was in the form of God, did not regard equality with God as something to be exploited but emptied himself, taking the form of a slave, being born into human likeness. And being found in human form, he humbled himself and became obedient to the point of death — even death on a cross" (Phil 2:6-8).

It is a reiterated theme in the Franciscan tradition that Francis linked the life of poverty, under the rubric of self-emptying, with the cross as the paradigmatic example of dying in humility and poverty. It did not escape those who studied the life of Francis to view his passion for poverty within the framework of the passion of Christ. Dante seems to have understood this perfectly well. In the eleventh canto of the *Paradiso* when Saint Dominic praises Francis, he says that at Calvary Mary stood at the foot of the cross but Lady Poverty climbed up the cross to embrace Jesus in his death.

Dante may or may not have known the allegorical text called the *Sacrum Commercium* (the "Sacred Exchange") written more than a decade after the death of Francis. That text makes the strongest case possible for the Franciscan understanding of poverty and does so using the example of nudity. Francis, searching for Lady Poverty, queries two ancients (representing the Old and New Testament?) about her location only to be told that she lives on top of a high mountain, and "if you wish to reach her, brother, take off your clothes of rejoicing and put aside every burden and sin clinging to you for, unless you are naked, you will not be able to climb to her who lives in so high a place" (chapter 11). When Francis does find Lady Poverty she is seated naked on a throne (chapter 15). In conversation with Francis she tells him that she walked nakedly with Adam in the garden of paradise before the Fall (chapter 25ff.). Toward the end of their long conversation and a simple meal of bread and water, Lady Poverty lays down to rest "naked upon the naked earth" (chapter 63) — an anticipation of Francis's own death when he asked to die naked on the ground close to Mother Earth.

This connection between nakedness and the cross and Franciscan poverty is a theme to which this study will return more than once. But as rich as that theme is in the subsequent life of Francis, it is anticipated in the scene between Francis and his father. Again, Thomas of Celano saw that in his description of the scene. Immediately after Guido wraps the young Francis in his vestment, Thomas interjects a homiletic cry: "Look! Now he wrestles naked with the naked!" In the very next chapter Thomas has Francis traveling about half naked — he who, as Thomas says, "once enjoyed wearing scarlet robes."

There is a passage in the recently discovered *Gospel of Thomas* that reflects the trope of spiritual nakedness: "The Disciples said: 'When will you be shown forth to us and when shall we behold you?' Jesus said: 'When you strip naked without being ashamed and take your garments and put them under your feet like little children and tread upon them, you will see the child of the living and not be afraid.'"

IT WAS CLEAR ENOUGH that Francis had "left the world" but it was not clear what he was going to do with his life. For the moment, in a kind of spiritual limbo of indecision, he did what he had been doing. He worked with lepers, he wandered about in prayer, and he continued with the physical work of rebuilding churches in the area. What he did, in fact, was to live like many of the spiritual outsiders — the "men of penance" as they were known — did: he prayed, he worked, he gave alms, he practiced the works of charity, and he looked for a sign. What that sign was to be he was not at all sure. In a sense, Francis lived providentially moving through the outskirts of Assisi.

When did all of these life-changing events take place? The early biographers of the saint were notoriously indifferent to strict chronologies, so readers of the early reminiscences must extrapolate from almost parenthetical asides. If we accept as accurate that Francis died twenty years after his conversion to Christ it would mean that at the time of his repudiation of his family patrimony he was roughly twenty-five, and since he died in 1226 these events happened around 1206.

In this period Francis did work with lepers in Gubbio for a time, but then returned to Assisi to continue his work of church rebuilding. The sources tell us that he did repairs not only on the church of San Damiano but also on the church of San Pietro and, in the valley below Assisi, on the chapel known as the "Little Portion" *(Portiuncula)*. That latter chapel would become, in time, the place that Francis favored as a center both for himself and for the band of followers who would join him. It had originally belonged to the Benedictines who had deep roots in the area of Assisi.

At this time in his life clothing again takes on importance. Francis assumed the clothing usually identified as that worn by hermits: he had a rough gown held at the waist by a leather belt, he wore shoes, and he carried a wooden staff. Many paintings of that period and later used such a costume to identify the typical hermit, the paradigmatic figure of whom was Saint Antony of the desert as conveyed through the powerful influence of Saint Athanasius's *Life of Saint Antony* in the fourth century.

The hermit's life was a common form adopted by those who had left the world to take up a life of prayer and penance. The hagiographical tradition is full of stories of men and women who went off to forests or deserts or mountains to live a life of solitude, poverty, and simplicity. It was a life that said symbolically that the person had fled from the world and the world's concerns. While some hermits graduated to that state after years of the common life of monastic living (Saint Benedict's *Rule*, for example, did not look with general favor on the eremitic life), there was a long tradition of "free-lance" hermits who adopted the life after a religious conversion. Creating a hermitage was a popular choice from the century before Francis as one way to live out the gospel life. Saints like Peter Damien, John Gualbert, and Bruno of Cologne all attempted to regularize the hermit life in this period. Francis himself always kept a love for eremetical retreat — as do Franciscans to this day.

The oldest tradition of the hermit life both in the deserts of the East and in the spirituality associated with Ireland, Scotland, and the British Isles was preeminently a lay phenomenon. Persons would simply move to a life of solitude out of a desire for solitude and a need for the simple life of prayer. Sometimes, such hermits would take up occupations like that of a river ferryman to make a living (the legend of Saint Christopher has him leading a solitary life as a river crossing person), while others lived as forest gleaners, part-time herders, or small-crop farmers.

This kind of free-form eremitical life seemed to have suited Francis's circumstances, since he needed some kind of identification in order to follow his still flexible plan to serve lepers, repair churches, and lead a life of prayer. What he sought out was a fairly common style of life adopted by many in the eleventh and twelfth centuries as an experiment in gospel living.

Francis followed this program for about two years. He then received an insight that set him on a new and radically different path. In 1208 on the feast of Saint Matthias, February 28, Francis listened to the proclamation of the Gospel and, unsure if he understood correctly, asked for the passage to be read to him again after Mass. The priest read it to him line for line: Jesus commanded his disciples to possess neither gold nor silver nor money, to carry neither a wallet nor a sack nor bread, and not to wear shoes but simply to go forth and proclaim the Good News (Mt 11:7-10).

That reading struck Francis as a direct inspiration: this is what he would do with his life. He heard the words of Jesus as a program for his life. When he heard those words, Thomas of Celano says, he heard them as no "deaf hearer." He immediately took off his shoes, unloosened the belt from his tunic replacing it with a simple cord, and set aside his staff. He then, Thomas continues, chalked a cross on the back of his tunic. Francis became, as it were, a cross bearer — a person who took up the cross not as a crusader in the military sense but as one who would be protected by the cross. He made this tunic very plain and poor and rough (Thomas uses all those words) so that the world would not covet it.

A contemporary Franciscan commentator, Paul LaChance, has written of the "conversions" of Saint Francis; the plural noun is quite apposite. In this early period of his life we can see three such conversions. He converted from a life of luxury and frivolity by converting to the service to the lepers. That conversion was the symbolic repudiation of his father's world. He then took up the life of penance and work symbolized by his hermit's habit of belt, shoes, and staff. When he heard, really heard, the gospel, he set aside that life and began his new life as an itinerant lay preacher, dependent on providence, in order to follow the poor Christ.

The stages Francis went through are hardly original with

him. From the end of the eleventh century there had been a strong reforming impulse in the church to combat the persistent problem of corruption in the church. That reforming impulse had as its background a compelling question: what is the gospel life or, as it was sometimes phrased, the apostolic life? The question, as is clear, was an attempt to get back to the absolute basics — a kind of *ressourcement* — in order to provide a purified way of living as a Christian, an attempt to re-form the church by reforming its members.

The answer to the question of what constituted the gospel life was various. Monks, and reforming impulses within monasticism, pointed to the church described in the Acts of the Apostles where the primitive community held all things in common. From that template they deduced that the most perfect form of the gospel life was the life of monasticism. Others decided that the best way of undercutting the corrupt life of the clergy would be to have the clergy live in community under a rule in order to serve the church effectively. Thus, the "Canons Regular" provided an alternative to monastic living. One of the most well known of the Canons was Hugh of Saint Victor who taught that if such clergy lived in community, relinquishing private possessions and exercising a life of humility, that combination — poverty and humility — would create a cadre of *Pauperes Christi* (The "Poor of Christ") who would be transformed into a life of charity: love of God and neighbor.

To those more "regular" experiments one must also note figures, especially in the early twelfth century in France, like Robert of Abrissel (died 1117) who combined a life of poverty with a life of itinerant preaching, a way of life formally endorsed in 1096 by Pope Urban II. Vitalis of Savigny (died 1122) followed the same pattern, although he added to it the apostolate of alleviating the suffering of the poor and the outcast by founding hospices for lepers, arranging marriages for fallen women (rather than clapping them into monasteries of women), finding shelter for the homeless, and so on. The most famous of these apostolic figures was Saint Robert of Xanten (died 1134), the founder of an order of Canons Regular in Premontre still extant today, who was an itinerant preacher with a special mission to preach peace and reconciliation to warring factions in towns and villages. When he did reluctantly accept the role of abbot for regular canons in Lyons he did so only on condition (the terms are important here) that they become "imitators of Christ" who "lived by the Gospel principle" and practiced "voluntary poverty."

Along with these attempts to breathe new life into clerical and monastic institutions there were also a number of lay initiatives, like the lay movement in the environs of Milan called the Patarines who resisted the corrupt clergy and feudal bishops in order to live a simple life of sharing and prayer, or the Hirsau reform in Germany in which laypeople attempted to live a lay life inspired by monastic ideals in their own homes. Their form of life actually received papal approval in 1091 by Urban II as part of his own efforts to reform the church.

The most famous movement in this period — a movement that bore some resemblance to what Francis was attempting to do — was inspired by a rich layman named Peter Waldo who gave up his rich life in Lyons in 1171 to live a life of poverty and itinerant preaching. Peter Waldo soon attracted a rather large following who preached in the area around Lyons. Their way of life received approval from Pope Alexander during the deliberations of Lateran III (1179) but the pope refused to give them a license to preach because of their lack of intellectual formation. They did not observe this restriction for long, and by 1184 they came under ecclesiastical censure. Their response was to insist that the "true church" derived from the apostolic life and not from apostolic succession. Some of their members veered into heresy, and a few actually seemed to have been touched by the Cathar heresy then deeply rooted in the culture of the south of France.

The movement of reforming laypersons in Lombardy, known as the Humiliati, had an evolution not unlike that of the Waldensians. Pope Innocent III gave them, not a rule, but a program *(propositum)* of life for the various strata of their membership (they actually had three orders within the movement). One rather striking part of their life was that instead of alms they shared the profit of their labors (they were mainly weavers by trade) with those in need. They also eventually got permission to listen to exhortations by their own members on Sunday which was, as Duane Lapsanski and other scholars have noted, a significant concession relative to the issue of who could preach and under what conditions. The Humiliati were groping toward some kind of life in which all classes could share in the gospel life with their insistence that ordinary lay life and work were compatible with the reforming impulses once almost exclusively found within the traditional religious orders or their reforming offshoots.

It is against that background that the life of Saint Francis must be understood as his life turned from his solitary search to follow the gospel life into a movement that had models and antecedents in the culture of his time. In other words, while

Francis is a singular figure, what he did and where he came from and what resources were at his disposal were not unique to him. Francis was not some solitary flower blooming in a desert. Attempts to portray Francis as a singular figure who invented something absolutely new — and such attempts are rife in the popular literature on him — oversimplify matters. That oversimplification, in turn, leads to an inability to see Francis within a larger tradition of Catholic reform and spirituality, and that, I think, is a very bad mistake. Such an oversimplification, as we shall see, also makes it extremely difficult to understand some of Francis's writings and many of the decisions he makes or the wishes he wants observed. If one does not see Francis within the stream of Catholic reform one does not see him clearly at all.

CHAPTER TWO

Francis and His Companions

*After the Lord gave me some brothers, no one showed me
what I had to do. . . .*

The Testament of Saint Francis

IN THE SPRING of 1208 some men of Assisi joined Francis to
follow in his way of life. They were an eclectic group. Bernard
of Quintavalle came from a wealthy family; Sylvester was a
priest of Assisi who had previously scorned Francis and his do-
ings; Giles and Peter and Philip are known to us mainly by
name. What does it mean to say that they "joined" him? Francis himself had no real plan of life other than his determined
effort to follow the example of the poor Christ, serve the needy,
work with his hands, and flee the secular world. At this early
stage it would be premature to speak of a religious "order" in
any canonical sense of the term. As he wrote in his *Testament,*
no one showed him what he had to do. Evidently, Francis sent
his companions out on little preaching missions with the understanding that they would come back for periodic meetings
at the Portiuncula — that little plot of land and chapel owned

by the Benedictine monks of Mount Subasio but given first on loan to Francis and then to the possession of Francis and his companions. At this stage of their existence they were little more than a like-minded group of pious penitents seeking a way of life but who, for now, simply acted in an ad hoc fashion.

By early 1209 a few more joined this little band so that their number was the highly symbolic twelve (whether we can trust that number can be left to the historians). It was quite one thing for Francis or Francis and a companion to be itinerant lay preachers living on the bounty of strangers, but it was quite another thing to have a dozen members in the community. With that number some need for structure was inevitable: when would the group gather for prayer? would they follow the canonical hours of the liturgy (Sylvester the priest would have had that obligation)? would they eat together? with what food and how supplied? As intuitive as Francis might have wished to stay, there was a certain inevitable need for a regularization of their life. That need became all the greater as the size of the fraternity increased in number.

Francis also knew that many ad hoc groups abroad had fallen into heretical practices or were under the suspicion of church authorities. Such had already become the case with groups like the Poor Men of Lyons (the Waldensians) and the Humiliati who had run afoul of Rome over issues like lay preaching and their understanding of sacramental powers. Consequently Francis decided, in the late spring of 1209, to take his eleven companions and go to Rome to get approval for their way of life and sanction for their activities from the pope, the powerful Innocent III, the former Lothario of Segni who had been elected pope as a thirty-seven-year-old cardinal deacon in 1198.

Innocent was a formidable figure who brought the papacy to its apex of power in the middle ages. It was Innocent who developed the claim that the pope possessed the fulness of power in both the spiritual and temporal realm; it was he who assumed the title "Vicar of Christ" as that which was appropriate for, and peculiar to, the pope alone. Before that time the popes were simply known as the "Vicar of Peter" since among their most fundamental tasks was to be guardians of the tomb of the apostle to whom Jesus entrusted the keys of the kingdom. Trained in canon law and theology, he organized anew the papal chancellery. He developed laws to coalesce jurisdictional powers to himself.

When Francis and his followers went to Rome the pope had many pressing issues on his mind. The Fourth Crusade (1202-04) to free the holy places from the Muslims had been a failure, but the pope single-mindedly sought to create a new crusading army. The church was in dire need of reform, which would lead him, in 1213, to call yet another general council to his palace in the Lateran — a council that would convene in 1215. The increased militancy of heretical groups in general and the Cathars of southern France in particular were a major worry. The flood of petitions for either ecclesiastical privileges or the settlement of legal grievances took up vast amounts of papal energy while giving a handsome living to the ever-swelling army of papal attendants living in Rome.

In preparation for that visit with the pope Francis wrote a simple rule of life to present to the pope for his approval, even though an earlier Lateran Council had decreed that there were only three monastic rules (those of Saints Basil, Benedict, and Augustine) to be used in the church. Francis managed to get an audience with the pope through a chain of intermediaries: the bishop of Assisi introduced Francis to the cardinal bishop of Albano, John of Saint Paul, who then got Francis to see the pope. In fact, we do not know what this early rule of Francis looked like at all. It might even be incorrect to call it a "rule" in the technical sense of the term. It most likely was more in the form of a schema (Latin: *propositum*) indicating how this little band proposed to live. Based on a careful reading of a rule written by Francis in 1221 (known as the "non-sealed rule" [*regula non-bullata*] because it did not get the papal stamp of approval), we can surmise that the document Francis brought to the pope was little more than a catena of scriptural texts indicating their desire to live in poverty, to practice penance, and to preach to the ordinary people.

The early Franciscan sources surround this desire for papal approval with a series of rather baroque incidents involving the pope having dreams of a ragged figure holding up the crumbling church or the pope sending Francis packing only to receive him because of a prophetic dream — not to mention Francis's willingness to actually live in a pigsty when the pope, in a moment of pique, told him to do so when first laying eyes on him. Most of these incidents were retrospective touches to show the fidelity of Francis to the pope and his curia as well as the pope's providential role in the founding of the order. These pious embroideries should not blind us from the one important fact, which is that the pope saw something in Francis and gave him *oral* permission to take up his way of life for himself and his companions. The intricacies of these negotiations may, in fact, mask the uncertainty with which the papal court reacted in the face of this ragged band of penitents.

Evidently the pope was won over by the argument of Cardinal John of Saint Paul that to deny them their way of life was to go against the words of the gospel, which plainly stated that the life of the disciple includes a life of poverty dedicated to preaching the way of penance and conversion. After all, Innocent himself had written a widely read treatise on the misery of the human condition and the need for conversion *(De Miseria Humanae Conditionis)* when he was still a cardinal. That argument only echoes a commonplace that had been in discussion for over a hundred years in Christendom: how does one go about living the gospel life? What was the paradigm? To what "canon within the canon" of sacred scripture would one appeal?

Saint Bonaventure, in his major life of Francis, desiring to emphasize the orthodoxy of these early friars, noted that the pope had the lay members of the group tonsured (thus, indicating that they belonged to the clerical state) and gave them permission to preach penance to the people while "promising them more in the future." Was it also during this time that Francis was ordained a deacon? We know for a fact that he was an ordained deacon (but never a priest) for the sources tell us that. When he was ordained to that order we really do not know, but this would have been a plausible moment for it to have happened. With that oral approval and the added permission to preach Francis distanced himself from any identification with lay groups like the Poor Men of Lyons who assumed the role of preaching (which meant, in essence, to explicate the scriptures in depth) contrary to the discipline of the church. Even with the approbation of the pope in hand, Francis always proceeded cautiously by asking permission of the local bishop to preach in his diocese. From the beginning,

Francis aligned his work within the boundaries of the hierarchical church.

If the meeting with the pope happened in late 1209, what we can then deduce is that by the year following the band of friars (friars merely meaning "brothers") had settled permanently at the Portiuncula. The early sources refer to this group simply as a *religio* — a "religion" (from the Latin *religare* — to bind) which, in the usage of the day, meant those who adopted a certain way of religious observance. How can we describe that *religio?* Quite simply, it was a mixed community of laypersons and priests who had dedicated themselves to a life of poverty, a willingness to identify themselves with the poor and the outcast, a mission of popular preaching, a tendency toward itinerancy but with another impulse toward periods of retirement, and a robust resistance to the acquisition of goods, incomes, properties, and endowments. They desired to work for their living or, when work was not available, to beg for alms. Francis would send them out in pairs, in obedience to the gospel model of disciples going abroad "two by two" to preach in the villages and towns.

The shape of this early group is a bit of a puzzle. Saint Francis called the group a "fraternity" (the word occurs ten times in his own writings). We also see the word *religio* in the early sources; sometimes they identify themselves as an "order of penitents," and at other times they are simply called "the brothers." The precise character of their canonical standing went through various permutations as the number of followers of Francis increased and their relationship to the larger church became an issue.

This style of life had certain novelties that marked the

religio of Francis off from the usual forms of religious life. Their emphasis on itinerancy was one. Unlike monks who vowed to live a stable life in a monastery for life, the friars were frequently "on the road." As Chesterton once said in a now famous aphorism: "What Benedict stored, Francis scattered." Unlike the clergy who maintained their life by the revenues derived from endowments, the friars would live from the work of their hands or, in times of need, by alms. It must be remembered that begging for alms was forbidden to the clergy as unseemly; they depended on incomes from fixed sources like tithes or endowments derived from possession of properties. When the friars went door to door asking for charity or begged in front of the churches of the towns and cities, they were crossing a social line that up to their time had been firm. "At that time," the *Legend of the Three Companions* insisted, "No one dared to give up their riches and their possessions and ask for charity door to door."

Their dress was simply the clothing of the very poor. It had no distinctive color; the use of brown, grey, or even green cloth was determined, not by rule, but by what was the cheapest cloth available. In England, for example, they came to be known as the "grey friars." They did adopt a distinctive style of dress to use as a social marker; their habit said something new since they did not adopt the typical habit of the monk nor that of the canon or the hermit. Their plain dress of gown with hood, cinched with a rope, was a sign of who they were. They either went barefoot or wore simple sandals.

The next few years saw Francis and his companions alternatively following the life of travel (Francis may have gone to Dalmatia in this period in a thwarted attempt to reach the

Muslim lands in order to preach and expose himself to the danger of martyrdom) and regular returns to the Portiuncula. On Palm Sunday evening in 1209 Clare Offreduccio, of the aristocratic family of the same name, came to Francis at the Portiuncula aspiring to live a life inspired by Francis's life of poverty. A great deal of romantic blather has been read into this encounter of the then eighteen-year-old young woman meeting the then twenty-eight-year-old man of penance. The very reticence of the early sources about their relationship may tell, in an oddly negative way, that they were great friends — a friendship that the sources may have wished not to emphasize overly much.

Recent writers such as Marco Bertoli, Ingrid Peterson, and Margaret Carney have been determined to see Clare in her own right and not merely as a star-struck adolescent who became infatuated with the example of Francis. That approach is surely correct. There is some evidence to suggest that Clare and the other women of her family, including her sisters, already had a vigorous spiritual life in their own home not unlike that of the medieval Beguines in the north. Witnesses at her canonization process (the proceedings of that process are extant) who knew her before her conversion mention her care for the poor, her life of prayer, her simplicity of life. She went with her mother on pilgrimage to Rome and to the shrine of the Archangel Michael at Monte Gargano in southern Italy. Her mother seems to have been an inveterate pilgrim who had visited the famous shrine of Campostela and also the holy places in Palestine. Clare wore modest clothes and, some testified, had resisted the idea of marriage in order to live a virginal life of prayer. Clare, in other words, came to the Portiuncula with a strong sense of

Christian discipleship and a formed spiritual maturity beyond her years. Clare thus underwent two conversions. She turned from an already pious life of Christian observance in a domestic setting toward the new vision that Francis and his companions offered. That this life of piety was first conducted within the confines of her own family would have been the rule and not the exception given the social standards of the day.

There was no question, however, of her taking up the mendicant life after the manner of the friars. Such a way of living would have been uthinkable in this period when women were expected to live within the shelter of the home or the convent. On that Palm Sunday evening Francis cut off Clare's hair as a sign of her withdrawal from the world; those shorn tresses are displayed in Assisi to this day. Francis had Clare go to a nearby Benedictine monastery but, within a month or so, after another short stay in another religious house, settled her at a house next to the rebuilt church of San Damiano. Eventually she set up her convent there, which became the home of her *religio* as it is to this day. What Clare insisted on, however, was that her companions (she was soon joined by her mother and two of her sisters) were to lead a religious life without having endowments or lands or other ordinary sources of income characteristic of monastic life at that time.

Clare determined to live purely on alms given to her community or by the work of their hands. This boldly risky enterprise was at the center of her understanding of religious life, but it was not until 1228, two years after the death of Francis, that this "privilege of poverty" *(privilegium paupertatis)* for three convents in Assisi was granted by the pope. This privilege did not come without difficulty since church authorities could not understand how such a community could exist without some ready source of support. Part of the story of Clare and her community inevitably deals with the degree to which her understanding of poverty was to be protected from well meaning attempts to modify it. Although over the years there would be modifications and compromises (but not in Clare's lifetime!) the Poor Clares give witness to this day of the intuitions of Clare and her companions.

Clare outlived Francis by over a quarter of a century. She lived to see her communities spread over a good part of Europe. From her cloister in Assisi she became an influential mistress of the spiritual life, serving as an advisor to popes and a protector of the city of Assisi. The particular genius of Clare was to discover a way in which she could live out the Franciscan insight of poverty for the sake of Christ in a manner possible for the women of her time. During the lifetime of Francis they kept in close contact. In the basilica of Saint Francis one can see, among the relics from the life of Francis, a plain woven white gown she sewed for the saint in his final illness. A text, discovered only in the twentieth century, addressed to the *poverelle* (the "Poor Ladies") has Francis begging them "to use with discernment the alms the Lord gives you" thus underscoring the concern with poverty that Francis, like Clare, saw as central to their way of life.

From the pen of Clare we have a series of four letters that she wrote to Agnes of Bohemia, daughter of that country's king, who wishes to model a convent in Prague after the manner of San Damiano. One other letter and her *Rule* round out the authentic writings of the saint. Whether the testament attributed to her or a blessing bearing her name are authentic is a matter of some scholarly debate. In the sixth chapter of her *Rule* Clare pays witness to the example and teaching of Francis as the inspiration for her own way of life. Within that same chapter are two excerpts from Francis's own teaching for the Poor Ladies. Francis promises "for myself and for my brothers always to have that same loving care and solicitude for you as I have for them." The *Rule* also quotes an exhortation of the dying Francis that the Poor Ladies should always keep their life of poverty and "keep most careful watch that you never depart from this by reason of the teaching or advice of anyone."

Clare is not often mentioned in the writings of Francis or in the early legends. She mentions him in her writings more frequently; she needed his authority as a founder to sustain her own form of life in poverty. One intriguing source mentions that Francis consulted her through an intermediary about his desire to take up the life of a hermit. We also know that he spent his last days ill and discouraged in a hut near San Damiano. What does seem to be the case is that Francis and Clare had one of those great spiritual friendships in which their mutual gifts were such to sustain the inspirations they had to live out their intuitions about the gospel life. In that sense, they are paired as naturally as Saint Teresa of Avila and Saint John of the Cross, Saints Francis de Sales and Jeanne Marie De Chantal, Saints Vincent de Paul and Louise de Marillac, or Peter Maurin and Dorothy Day in our own day.

In the lifetime of Francis it might be premature to assume two "orders" of Franciscans — that of the friars and that of the sisters. It might be more correct to speak of a movement of people intending to lead a more intense Christian life with the concomitant desire to privilege a life of poverty. Over some decades, through clarification and the adoption of a regular life (which is to say, life under a rule), this movement became two orders. It is the task of the historian of these matters to pinpoint precisely when this solidification came about, but it certainly was happening, in the case of the friars at least, toward the end of Francis's life.

But what about the laypeople? When did the so-called "third order" take shape? The answer to that question is not an easy one. We know from the sources that some people in Assisi and elsewhere thought that the little fraternity of penitents were layabouts or insane. Others listened closely to what the followers of Francis and Francis himself had to say. Many of these people, however, could not simply leave home and hearth to take up a mendicant life. They may have had obligations to family or to their social network. To those people Francis had to provide some spiritual advice to lead, more intensely, a Christian way of being in the world.

In two versions of a letter of exhortation written to "all people" (written perhaps less than ten years before he died) we may get verification of this more general style of life that Francis preached to people. It is not clear to whom these letters (more properly, exhortations) were addressed. Were they for all Christians or for all those who had taken up the penitential life? The salutation is ambiguous, but the main themes are clear. One can detect in them two distinct but interwoven messages.

First, Francis wanted those who heard his preaching to lead a Catholic life. He insisted clearly that a good Christian life demanded reverence and reception of the eucharist; that this eucharistic piety presupposed the regular confession of sins; that priests were to be honored and churches visited. In all of those emphases there was an implied rebuke to the Cathars who did not hold to an orthodox view of the sacraments and the Waldensians who resisted the notion that true Christianity rested not in the authority of Holy Orders but in the purity of the believing community itself. If there is one thing that is not new, original, or radical in the mind of Francis it is his understanding of sacramental theology. His instructions are quite obviously inspired by the teachings of the Fourth Lateran Council.

The second great theme was his great catechetical instruction on Jesus Christ who is, in Francis's words, the one who was the Word of God who "received the flesh of our humanity and frailty." It is that same Christ who lived a life of poverty, who further humbled himself in the sacrament of the eucharist and through the cross, who is the exemplar for us. From that supremely orthodox christology — again, an implied rebuke to the Cathars — Francis deduces that our salvation comes from receiving this Christ "with heart pure and our body chaste." In other words, he invites people to convert to Christ and, in that conversion, fruits of penance will come. Those fruits are love of neighbor, alms for the poor, charity to all, and a spirit of humility.

When one looks carefully at this exhortation, it is clear that Francis had a vision for Christian living that had deep roots in ecclesial life modeled on the meaning of the Incarnate Christ. Francis sees this form of Christian living as a deeply relational reality that intertwines Christ, church, and society. He puts it brilliantly:

We are spouses when the faithful soul is united by the Holy Spirit to our Lord Jesus Christ. We are brothers, moreover, when we do the will of the Father who is in heaven; mothers when we carry Him in our heart and body through love and a pure and sincere conscience; and give Him birth through a holy activity, which must shine before others by example.

In the years between 1212 and 1215 we have a movement beginning to take shape. Francis has an increasing number of brothers who go out to preach and then return for periods of solitude and for common discussion. The women who have joined Clare are situated in convents where they lead a life of prayer sustained by alms granted by the local populace. There are also persons who, inspired by the gospel vision preached by the Lesser Brothers, ally themselves to the way of life preached by Francis. Ordinary laypeople would be attracted to the convents to ask for prayers, receive spiritual instruction, and so on. This was their role in the more general reformation of the culture. It would only be in the future that more canonical stipulations, in the form of recognized rules of life, would give more order and coherence to what is still in an embryonic state.

We are fortunate that there are some contemporary witnesses to the work inspired by Francis. The most valuable of these testimonies comes from the pen of Jacques de Vitry (died 1240) who had occasion to see the Lesser Brothers at their preaching. De Vitry wrote a letter back to his companions in his hometown of Liege before his departure to take up the bishopric of Acre in the Crusader States. He tells how the

Lesser Brothers and the Lesser Sisters were held in esteem by the papal curia for their way of life. He goes on:

> They live according to the form of the primitive church. . . . During the day they go into the cities and villages giving themselves over to the active life in order to gain others; at night, however, they return to their hermitage or solitary places to devote themselves to contemplation. The women dwell together near the city in various hospices, accepting nothing, but living by the work of their hands. They are grieved, indeed troubled, by the fact that they are honored by both clergy and laity more than they would wish.

There are a number of highly interesting things to note in that brief paragraph. First, De Vitry explicitly notes that their "form" of life is that of the primitive church — a "form" that had been sought after by reforming elements going back at least to the papacy of Gregory VII. Second, the Lesser Brothers are said to combine the twin activities of action (during the day) and contemplation (during the night), so that the old distinction between the active and the contemplative is now replaced by the so-called "mixed life" *(vita mixta)* that became more prominent in this period. Jacques de Vitry also notes that the women "accepted nothing," which, of course, means that they resisted the older monastic paradigm of receiving endowments or dowries or vested properties, preferring to work by their hands (we know, for example, that needlework and spinning were frequent occupations) or, although the letter does not say it explicitly, to receive alms. De Vitry's description points to the fact that he drew upon a vocabulary that had been current for some time before the advent of Francis.

Nonetheless, Jacques de Vitry understood that what this movement was doing was something quite new. He was well acquainted with the Beguines in the north who worked out a way for women to live in small urban communities without formally entering religious life. He devoted a chapter to the Franciscans in his great work on the Latin Church *(Historia Occidentalis)*. In Chapter 32 of that book he said that up to this time in the life of the church there were three religious orders: monks, hermits, and canons. In our time, he said, the Lord lifted up a fourth order or, to be more precise, renewed something that had been the form of the primitive church of the Acts of the Apostles; his textbook case for this new way was the movement started by Brother Francis, "a simple, uneducated man beloved by God and man." Jacques de Vitry goes on to single out certain innovative characteristics of this new movement. He records that these Lesser Brothers are free of any property either in the form of monastery complexes and churches or sources of income like vineyards or domestic animals or fields. He goes on to note that the Lesser Brothers invite men from both the lower orders and "high born nobles" to dispossess themselves, which, he says, they do by girding themselves with a rope around a cheap tunic with a hood.

The idea of freedom from class distinction is, according to the *Historia Occidentalis,* one reason for their expansive growth. He says that the only men excluded from their order are those who are married and those who have made a promise (a vow?) to join another religious order. The growth of the movement was undeniable since, as De Vitry notes, there is "scarcely a kingdom in Christendom" that does not have a representative number of these brothers.

In the period between Clare's visit to Francis on Palm Sunday 1212 and Francis's visit to Rome in 1215 a number of things happened that would play out in important ways in the subsequent history of Francis and his brothers. A noble lord, Count Leo, gave Francis the use of a mountain near the Tuscan town of Arezzo, called La Verna, that he would use for a hermitage. That place would play a significant role in the last years of his life. In the same period (1213? 1214?) Francis attempted a journey to Spain with the idea of again preaching to Muslims either in their Iberian territories or across the Mediterranean in Morocco, but that journey did not succeed and he returned to Italy. Francis's desire to preach to the Muslims would be fulfilled in the next decade both by himself and by the first friars making their way to Morocco, but his two early attempts in these years came to naught.

The tug of the Islamic world must be seen against the background of the crusading spirit in which Christian Europe attempted by force of arms to wrest the Holy Places from "pagan" hands. In these years of Francis's life there had already been four crusading attempts. The crusades were motivated not only by the restoration of the holy places but also by the attempt to keep the Muslim world at bay. The anti-Muslim spirit was deeply woven into the culture of Europe as early medieval epic poems like "The Song of Roland" so vividly show. Islam and Islamic forces were never far from the minds of medieval Christians. Despite some benign contact between these two cultural forces (in Sicily; in Spain) it is worth noting that three generations after the death of Francis, when Dante described the walls of the City of Dis in hell, he describes them as like the fiery turrets of mosques. Mohammad himself lies mutilated in the ninth circle of hell punished as a sower of schism and scandal. Next to him is his son-in-law Ali, the fourth in line of succession after Mohammad. Medieval legend had it that Mohammad was an apostate Christian (sometimes described as a former cardinal!) who rent the Christian world.

Interestingly enough, Francis, a quondam knight, now sees his vocation to go to the Islamic world and preach his characteristic message of peace and the truth of the gospel. Given the bellicose fever of the time it was a rather quixotic approach, but it was an approach in which Francis had invested his whole soul. He also saw this as an opportunity for martyrdom which would count as a supreme example of following Christ who gave up his life. Some centuries later the young Teresa of Avila would have the same dream — to go to the Muslim lands and risk martyrdom in the name of the gospel. In the somewhat fevered religious imagination of the times Islam meant martyrdom.

In 1215 Francis took his little band to Rome to be present when the hierarchs of the church gathered at the Lateran Palace for the fourth time to hold a council for the reform of the church — a council called by the pope who had given approval to his way of life, Pope Innocent III. He spent his time with the poor swarms of beggars outside the churches or gathering news about what the deliberations inside the Lateran were all about. The trip to Rome was not only an act of piety toward the church but also an opportunity to be part of the plan to invigorate the life of the church, albeit with little chance that this still small band would have a direct part to play in the formal proceedings.

CHAPTER THREE

Rome and Beyond Rome

This sacred synod imparts the benefit of its blessings to all who set out on this common enterprise. . . .

The Lateran Council (1215)

IN THE WAKE of the papacy of Gregory VII (died 1085) there had been a series of general councils held in Rome all concerned with reform within the church. Retrospectively, these councils have been called "ecumenical," although in fact they are more properly understood as general or plenary councils in the West since the bishops of the Eastern church were either not in attendance at all or, at most, only sparsely represented. In fact, in our own day, Pope Paul VI has referred to these five councils held at the Lateran (the last was held on the eve of the Reformation in 1517) as "general councils of the West" to signal, however subtly, that he does not want to make a break with the Christian East, which recognizes only the first eight truly ecumenical councils. The distinction between general councils and ecumenical councils is an important one for ecumenical reasons but it also underlines the character of the various

Lateran Councils: they were oriented fundamentally to reformation within Western Christianity.

The first Lateran Council sat for only a month in 1123. The canons produced by that council reflect the general concern for reform of church structures. The buying of church offices (simony) was condemned; clerical concubinage was excoriated; the relationship of vowed religious to bishops was set out; the prohibition of marriage by monks, deacons, subdeacons, and priests was decreed. Lateran II, which met in 1139 during the month of April, made the same rulings as did provincial synods in Italy (Pisa) and France (Clermont and Rheims) in the same period.

Forty years later in March of 1179, Lateran III met with 500 bishops attending (only one came from the East). This council reiterated the reforming canons of the earlier councils (thus testifying to how persistent the issues were) and added some procedures for the elections of popes in order to rectify the unseemly recurrence of competing claimants to the papal throne that had been a regular feature of earlier elections. One further salient reform was instituted but, alas, never fully implemented. The council forbade the custom of people holding multiple benefices — those ecclesiastical offices endowed for the support of parish priests or abbots of monasteries from which accrued the monies for these endowed positions. Most often, in fact, those who held legal title to those endowments did not reside in the place or have a direct concern for the well being of the benefice. The failure to reform the abuses of the benefice system, again condemned at Lateran IV and later councils, would fester in the church as an open wound down to the early modern period.

When Pope Innocent III called for a council in 1213 he had behind him the church's experience with three previous reform councils that had met in the Lateran palaces in less than a century. When the council actually met in November 1215 there were in attendance over four hundred bishops while another 800 prelates attended as auditors. Some scholars have argued that Innocent personally set the agenda, and the council did nothing but vote on the canons he put forward. For our purposes these scholarly debates on the procedures of the council are beside the point. What is crucial is that Francis and some of his companions were in Rome when the council was held and, further, that Francis took very seriously the deliberations and conclusions contained in the canons of that council. Whether he actually attended any of the sessions is unknown.

The canons of Lateran IV were the most balanced and far reaching of all of the councils that met in Rome during this period. They ranged widely on a variety of subjects for which they made precise stipulations: from the usual canons against clerical abuse to the increased segregation of Jews from the larger society; on the relationship of the Greeks to the papacy delivered in a ham-handed manner that did little to mend the strained relations between East and West; on the need to prepare preachers better and for more education for clerics; on who was to preach and by what authority. The most important of the canons carried an implicit rebuke to heretical groups like the Cathars and the Waldensians: all Catholics were to confess their sins at least once a year and those same Catholics were to receive Holy Communion at least once annually. Lateran IV conveyed a "strong" doctrine of the sacrament of the eucharist and the real presence of Christ in the consecrated

elements of the bread and wine and an equally strong affirmation of priestly powers derived from the sacrament of holy orders, both of which were expressed in the opening statement of
faith that prefaces the particular canons adopted at the council.
In that opening of the acts of the council there is a firm statement of belief in the true presence of Christ in the eucharist,
the adoption of the technical language of transubstantiation,
and the requirement that no person except a priest who had
been properly ordained within the church can validly confect
this sacrament.

Those affirmations were made as a statement against the
heretical opinions of those groups who were bitterly critical of
the priesthood as a whole. The annual "Easter Duty" (as it
came to be called) of requiring confession made to a priest
once a year and holy communion to be received from his hands
during the Easter season had more influence, according to
some historians, on keeping Christian identity intact than any
other legislation coming out of the council even when the stip-
ulation was not uniformly observed. Communion at Eastertide
was also a way of distinguishing orthodox Catholic believers
from their heretical brethren.

The reforming impulse deriving from the work of Gregory VII in the previous century had unleashed a long series of
experiments in how one was to live the *vita evangelica.* The cu-
mulative effect of the four councils held at the Lateran ended
up providing a broad portrait of who this Christian was: a person who lived the sacramental life of the church; one who fit
into the proper place within the hierarchical church; one who
freed oneself from the abuses that marred church life; one who
was a bearer of the cross (a crusader); one who held to the

unity of the church by the Catholic faith (professed as a prologue of the conciliar decrees) and eschewed the various here-
sies of the time. In other words, the work of the Lateran councils was to provide a framework within which the various
experiments in gospel living were to be lived out. In that sense,
Lateran IV provided a juridical framework within which experiments in "gospel living" were to be understood.

The corpus of Francis's own writings makes it clear that he
intended to live a life of poverty and penance but within the
boundaries of the Catholic faith. In Chapter 19 of the unconfirmed rule he states flatly: "Let all the brothers be, live, and
speak as Catholics." In the very next chapter he orders the friars
to confess to a priest in their order, but if one is not available,
they should confess to "other discerning and Catholic priests."
In his final letter to the faithful he admonishes the faithful to
"fast and abstain from vices and from an excess of food and
drink and be Catholics." "Catholic" in the vocabulary of Francis meant to live according to the belief and practice (*more
catholico* is the Latin phrase he uses: "according to the catholic
manner") of the great church under the authority of the pope.
The reiteration of the word "catholic" in the writings of Francis
is not without moment. At a very minimum the word was used
to distinguish his followers from any heterodox group active at
that time.

In a letter written to the entire order at a time close to his
death, there is a passage in which Francis exhorts the friars to
lives of conformity in faith. In the course of that letter he singles out a need to honor the holy eucharist. He goes on to plead
with priests that they be properly disposed when they say mass.
He gives solemn warnings to those who do not honor the

eucharist in a fitting manner. "Let everyone be struck with fear . . . when Christ, the Son of the Living God, is present on the altar in the hands of the priest." He stipulates that one mass a day is to be celebrated in a given house, that the members are to be careful with all liturgical objects and books, and that they are to celebrate the liturgical offices with devotion, harmony, and recollection. In a most solemn fashion, Francis ends these exhortations by saying, "I do not consider those brothers who do not wish to observe these things Catholics or my brothers; I do not even wish to see or speak with them until they have done penance."

The emphasis Francis puts on the eucharist cannot be fully explained by appealing to his reverence for church doctrine or his tacit repudiation of the various heretical sects of the time. Francis saw in the eucharist a continuation of something far more fundamental: the humility of Christ who took on flesh even though he was the Eternal Word. In the very first of his collected admonitions addressed at various times to his fraternity Francis makes the correlation explicit. He said that during his lifetime the disciples of Jesus saw him in the flesh by an "insight of their flesh" yet believed he was divine "as they contemplated him with their spiritual eyes." So, we now see bread and wine with our bodily eyes yet firmly believe that Christ's holy body and blood are present in the eucharist. What Francis states in this belief is a very old topos in the Christian tradition: possessing a mystical (in the deepest etymological meaning of "hidden") sense. The patristic tradition said that those who see beyond the text of the scriptures or the bread and wine on the altar or even the church itself intuit the hidden (that is, mystical) significance of those realities that go beyond the phenomenal realities perceived by the senses. That insight comes only from deep faith.

To understand the true meaning of the eucharist is similar to the way we "see" Christ in the poor: by a vision that penetrates beyond surface realities. There is a very real sense in which the mystery of the incarnation and the mystery of the eucharist are related to that ability to understand deeply what only appears on the surface to those who lack the eyes of faith.

In reading through Francis's writings (especially the writings from the last decade of his life) it is striking how often he returns to the same themes of the dignity of the priesthood, of the sacred mystery of the eucharist, of reverence for the physical plant of the church building, of veneration for the written word in general and the Word of God in particular; of the need for confession and penance; and of his protestations of orthodoxy. In other words, the very stipulations drawn from Lateran IV give tone to the fraternity he leads. Francis was a preacher of penance and renewal, but it was from within the Catholic Church that he wished reform to come.

About this picture of Francis as a supremely orthodox medieval Catholic (*pace* the tradition deriving from Paul Sabatier who wished to turn Francis into a simple evangelical Protestant) two points need to be made. The first is a simple one: nobody can attain an adequate understanding of Francis by reading only the *legenda* written about him. This is a point that current scholars make with increasing frequency: it is to the writings by Francis and not only those about him that serious students of the saint must go if they are to understand him. While many of the texts that come from Francis's pen are less than elegant and written for an *ad hoc* occasion, it is precisely in those writings that we get a clear picture of what issues were closest to his own desires and aspirations. A fair and unbiased reading of his writings gives no comfort to those who would like to edge him closer to the Poor Men of Lyons or the Humiliati and away from a firm place within the structures of the medieval church and its sacramental and judicial demands. Francis lived, to borrow one of his own phrases, *more catholico* — after the Catholic manner.

That being said, however, we cannot simply place him in some stereotypical category like "medieval saint" by a lack of nuance in reading about him. He was not simply "hewing a certain line" as an unblinkingly obedient automaton. Francis was not "typical." If he were, how does one explain the singular power of his person within his own lifetime and later? What makes him for us, as it did for his contemporaries, "untypical" was the rigor with which he attempted to flesh out what he learned from a profound meditation on the meaning of the gospel. What Francis understood was that the core meaning of Christianity did not come from following the New Testament as some kind of manual for spiritual perfection. The New Testament was a witness to the meaning of Jesus Christ. To be a disciple of Jesus was not to follow a doctrine but to imitate a person as that person is witnessed to in the Word of God. The continuing presence of the church in its attempt to do that is the context for this imitation (we can always look back into the tradition to see models about how to do this), but there are always far richer resources to find new ways and other angles to bring this imitation to fruition.

Within the half decade between the end of the fourth Lateran council in Rome and the year 1220 a number of quite important events occurred that affected both the life of Francis and the direction of the movement he inspired. On July 16, 1216, Pope Innocent III died. Jacques de Vitry, that indefatigable chronicler of life in his day, has a lugubrious account of how the pontiff's body was denuded by persons who stripped him of his pontificals and jewelry for profit as his body lay in state in Perugia where he succumbed to a fever while on a journey. Two days after his death, on July 18, the cardinals elected the aged cardinal priest of St. John and Paul, the great protector of Francis and his fraternity, who took the name of Honorius III. It was this pope who would give final approval to the mendicant order of preachers known as the Dominicans (1216), similar approval for the revised Franciscan rule in 1223, and for the Carmelites in 1226. Honorius, in short, set his seal of approval on these new movements, which distinguished themselves from the older monastic orders. All of these groups were mendicant: they begged for their support. Their particular emphases were also quite distinct. The Dominicans put their main focus on preaching; hence, their name, the Order of Preachers. The Carmelites had evolved from an eremitical foundation in the Holy Land whose impulses were mainly contemplative.

The Franciscans, then known as the Minor Brothers, in obedience to the decrees of Lateran IV, held regular chapters of their order. The most significant of these was the Pentecost chapter of 1217 that convened at the Portiuncula. By the time the order met again in 1221 the order had been divided into provinces with their own supervising ministers, and, if we can trust the numbers, three thousand friars attended that Pentecost meeting which, due to the rudimentary provisions for sleeping, has come down to us under the name of "the chapter of mats." It was at the 1217 Pentecost meeting, according to tradition, that Dominic Guzman (1170?-1221), the Spanish founder of the Order of Preachers (now more commonly called "Dominicans"), came to spend time with Francis.

Dominic Guzman had little of the charismatic appeal of Francis but he did have some gifts that Francis lacked — most notably, a clear sense of what his *religio* was to do (study and preach) and a good head for administration. Those gifts, and the fact that his order took on the well-established Rule of Saint Augustine, spared the preaching friars from the rancorous divisions that afflicted the Franciscans who looked to their founder to divine how religious life was to be lived. Dominic and Francis were friends and, touchingly enough, even though they were in some sense competitors, Dante has Thomas Aquinas praise Saint Francis in the *Paradiso* while Saint Bonaventure does the same for Saint Dominic.

It was at the Pentecost chapter of 1217 that it was officially decided to send friars on missionary journeys both beyond the Alps and into the world of Islam. The beloved Brother Giles left for Tunis while Brother Elias of Cortona (who would figure prominently in the later history of the order) went to Syria where Francis would meet him later when he himself journeyed to the Middle East. Francis himself decided to go to France but, while in Florence, Cardinal Ugolino persuaded him to remain in Italy. This emphasis to spread the influence of the friars gets its greatest impetus from the Pentecost meetings at the Portiuncula. Within less than a decade after the death of Francis we have independent witnesses attesting to the work of the Lesser Brothers in France, Germany, the Iberian peninsula, the Middle East, and in the British Isles.

The increasing number of friars attending the Pentecost chapters can be understood as both a tribute to the attractive power of the lesser brothers and a premonition of problems that would soon come into the open. It was one thing for Francis to act as a spiritual master and guide for a small band of loyal followers, but it was hardly possible for Francis, in person, to be a spiritual guide for three thousand brothers. The very growth of the order brought with it immediate issues: by what criteria were friars to be accepted into the group? Who was to do the screening of applicants and, more crucially, who was to form them into the way of life to which they had come? How were they to give theological instruction to those who were priests or who aspired to the priesthood? Lateran IV stipulates theological education for preachers and clergy. Where was this to be done? By whom? And further: how did one hold the need for infrastructure that such education and administration demanded in some kind of harmony with the rigid understanding of the poor life that was the rock-solid foundation on which Francis envisioned his life? These were practical considerations which Francis had neither the focus nor the interest to solve.

Not to put too fine a point on it: with the growth of the Lesser Brothers there came, almost as a necessary consequence, more structure, more material needs, and an inevitable reshaping of the vision of what the order was and how it was to carry out its task. This process has been described, in the language of the modern social sciences, as the "routinization of charisma," which is almost a necessary consequence of a social phenomenon that arises under the inspiration of a charismatic leader. The anxieties and sense of disappointment reflected in Francis's later writing, especially in the *Testament,* was a very human reaction to a very inevitable evolution. That evolution should not be judged as a betrayal of Francis but as the impossibility to duplicate a social structure totally faithful to the extraordinary gift of one person. Some scholars have argued that Francis effectively lost control of the whole order after the Pentecost chapter of 1217. One thinks of the cynical remark (not lacking in truth simply because it is cynical) of the nineteenth-century savant who said that Jesus came preaching the Kingdom of God and we ended up with the Catholic Church. Is it the case that Francis preached the humble following of Christ but ended up as the head of a vast religious order?

After another chapter held at the Portiuncula in 1219 some of the friars left to evangelize the Muslim world in Morocco. The following year five of them died as martyrs. Their death, among other things, inspired a Portuguese canon and theologian known to us as Anthony of Padua (1193?-1231) to join the Lesser Brothers. Anthony's decision to become a Franciscan added another dimension to the evolving shape of the movement. What was to be done with a friar who had an excellent theological education and evident gifts for preaching and writing? Would such a person have to submerge quite clear intellectual talents to join the poor brothers? Francis was not very enthusiastic about "book learning," but he did have great admiration for those who were theologians and/or commentators on the scriptures. In one of the very few private letters that we possess from his pen Francis wrote to Anthony some time around 1223 to indicate his approval for theological work: "I am pleased that you teach sacred theology to the brothers provided that, as it is contained in the Rule, you 'do not extinguish the Spirit of prayer and devotion' during study of this kind."

Anthony would outlive Francis and serve the order well in northern Italy. He composed a series of sermons on the Sunday readings as well as another series for the feast days of the liturgical year. It is on the basis of those writings that he was later declared a Doctor of the Church by Pope Pius XII in 1946. Those sermons are little read today by anyone but scholars, but this learned friar who combined study with simplicity and humility is one of the most popular of saints. In many places to this day people make contributions for "Saint Anthony's Bread" — offerings used to sustain the poor and the homeless. The basilica which houses his body in Padua is a popular destination for pilgrims and variations of his name are common among Catholics even to this day. Few, however, remember Anthony as a fine, if not first-rate, theologian in his own day.

Saint Francis, who had tried before to go to the Muslim world, finally made such a trip in 1219. He sailed from Ancona in June and made land shortly thereafter in Acre. He visited the friars who had gone to Syria and then proceeded to the Crusader camp outside of Damietta, which had been under siege for some time. The Crusader camp itself housed soldiers and mercenaries from twenty different European states who, variously, joined the crusade for either religious ideals or the promise of loot or the sheer joy of warfare. There was little in the way of overall leadership at the camp, and the forces were frequently riven into factions especially when tensions boiled over between the aristocratic knights (the *majores*) and the common foot soldiers *(minores)* — a problem that Francis would easily recognize given his own experiences in Assisi.

It is difficult to describe the brutality and sheer savagery of warfare in this period. One incident that occurred when Francis was in the camp must suffice. On August 16 a band of eight Saracen scouts were captured by the Christians. Their noses, arms, lips, and ears were cut off, and one eye was put out. Half of them were sent back to Damietta to warn, by their very appearance, the inhabitants what was to come when the walls were breached. The other scouts were hanged on the crusader fortifications as a salutary warning. Those poor men, in the words of a recent author, were "reduced to bloody scarecrows."

On November 5 the crusaders finally breached the walls of Damietta and entered the city to find a macabre scene. The city had been devastated by illness, lack of provisions, and the inability to bury the corpses. The dead had been savaged by packs of dogs, and the stench of death hung like a pall over the city. The long siege, the crusader blockade of those who had attempted to provision the city, and the deplorable hygiene inside the walls had turned the city into a veritable charnel house. The ruler himself, along with some of his troops, retreated south to take a stand against further incursions aimed at Cairo.

Either before the Christian victory over the city or later in the caliph's retreat headquarters (scholars are not of one mind over the chronology), Francis crossed the battle lines in order to speak to the caliph, Malik-al-Kamil. Some early Franciscan chroniclers say that he made the visit because he was horrified by the violence of the crusading army. Whatever the case may be, Francis did make such a visit in the company of Brother Illuminato, one of his early companions. Pilgrims can still see some tokens the sultan gave him, including a mounted ivory tusk, exhibited in the basilica of Saint Francis in Assisi. Jacques de Vitry, who was bishop of Acre but present at Damietta, tells us in his *Historia Occidentalis* that Francis spent a few days speaking and preaching in the court and that Malik-al-Kamil "listened attentively to Francis as he preached the faith in Christ to him and his followers." De Vitry says that the sultan saw Francis as a man of God but fearing his persuasive powers had him returned to the Christian camp with "reverence and security."

Some of the early sources say that Francis offered to go through an ordeal by fire if some of the Muslim holy men would do the same to see who was speaking the truth, but the sultan refused to allow such an encounter. The account of such a proposed encounter is actually depicted in one of the series of frescoes in the upper church of Saint Francis in Assisi. A much later account (in the fourteenth-century vernacular collection known as the *Fioretti*) actually has the sultan making a secret conversion, but that is most likely hagiographical wishing. Nor is it absolutely clear, as some have attempted to prove, that Malik-al-Kamil was a member of the Sufi brotherhood which, if true, might explain why Francis was so graciously received, since the Sufis had strong mystical tendencies with a concomitant reverence for holy men and a mystical practice of adoring God as love. The Sufi emphasis on union with Allah out of love may have made Malik-al-Kamil respectful of this Western holy man. Whatever the case may be, it does help to explain the epitaph on the Cairo grave of a Muslim scholar and confidant of the sultan which says that he had an "adventure with a Christian monk."

Scholars dispute many aspects of this famous encounter

and different voices gave different interpretations of the event. What seems indubitable, however, is that Francis gave an example that was rare enough in his day. At a time when violence was the rule of the day he dared cross enemy lines at the risk of painful death in order to speak face to face with someone who was demonized by the crusaders. Moreover, this was one of the few times that a Christian actually confronted a Muslim not with arms but with nothing more than Christian intentions of evangelization. One could say that Francis gave an alternative understanding of the word "crusader" (Latin: *Crucifer;* Greek: *Christopheros*) — one who bears the cross.

Arnaldo Fortini, the former mayor of Assisi, noted biographer of the saint, and indefatigable student of the Assisi archives, wrote in his great work on the saint that something happened there at Damietta that interested his own contemporaries not at all: at the very time when two armies were trying to annihilate each other two great and noble spirits came to understand and love one another. The experience of Francis before the sultan's court was a representative example of the primitive Franciscan desire to be a witness in Muslim lands. In the same period that Francis sojourned in Egypt, five of his confreres were executed in Morocco, where they had gone to preach the gospel.

The example of Francis in the Middle East did inspire the Franciscans to make their presence known in that part of the world. To this day, the Franciscans are the Catholic custodians of many shrines and churches in the Holy Land where they minister both to the native Christian population and to the millions of pilgrims who travel there out of devotion.

Francis went on to the Holy Land for a pilgrimage to Jerusalem, which, apart from the Church of the Holy Sepulchre, was mostly in ruins. The greater area lay devastated due to the constant warring of the time. During this journey a simple friar named Stefano, who had been searching for him, delivered this simple message: "Return, Return! On account of the absence of Brother Francis the order is disturbed, torn asunder, and scattered." In the late spring of 1220 Francis landed in Venice after a year in the Middle East. His sojourn there may have made a great impression on him. In an open letter to all civil authorities he may have had the Muslim call to prayer in mind when he asked them that every evening "an announcement may be made by a messenger or some other sign that praise and thanksgiving may be given by all the people to the all-powerful Lord God."

CHAPTER FOUR

Francis and the Rule(s) of the Lesser Brothers

The Rule of these brothers is this: to live in obedience, in chastity, and without anything of their own and to follow the teachings and the footprints of Our Lord Jesus Christ.

Saint Francis of Assisi

WHEN SAINT FRANCIS returned from the Middle East after a year's absence it was clear that during that period he had not been in firm control of his order. He was too distant and preoccupied with other issues to follow closely the affairs of his brethren. It was at this time (or perhaps as early as the Pentecost chapter of 1217) that Francis ceded governance of his order to the friar Peter Catani who, alas, was to die in the early spring of 1221. It was in that same year that a new chapter was held at which two things of some moment occurred. First, Brother Elias of Cortona took over the order as minister general and, at the same time, a new rule was written to stipulate more clearly the character and discipline of the order. This new rule was to flesh out the original form of life presented to the pope for his approval a decade earlier.

That there was some necessity for a more precise rule is evident from a papal bull issued by Pope Honorius III *(Cum Secundum)* in early fall 1220. The pope condemned the practice of those who give away their earthly possessions, assume some kind of a penitential habit, and begin wandering from place to place. Such persons were under no kind of religious rule, had received no formation, and, inevitably, drew some who were either not stable persons or, worse, vagrants and mischief makers. For the good order of society and for the reform of religious enthusiasm, there had to be some kind of framework in which those who were attracted to the itinerant and mendicant life were shaped. Free-floating bands of religious zealots was a reality with which medieval society would have little sympathy. As a partial response to this need, the lesser brothers needed a clear rule of life.

The Rule of 1221 is commonly called the "unsealed rule" because it never got the final seal *(bulla:* the lead seal affixed to official papal documents; hence its Latin title *regula non-bullata).* We do have the text of that unconfirmed rule, and it is worthy of some attention. The actual text consists of a prologue followed by twenty-four chapters of varying length. Printed in a modern version it is less than twenty-five pages long. The first chapter enjoins chastity, obedience, and a life without personal possessions. The second describes how friars are to be received and clothed. The following chapters make certain stipulations about a regulated life in the community: the organization of superiors (to be called ministers and servants); work; resistance to receiving any money; the begging of alms; how to care for the sick; fraternal charity; leading a chaste life; etc. Friars are forbidden to ride horses (the mark of a certain social status); those who are so called may go among the Saracens but not to engage in "disputes or arguments" but simply to proclaim the Word of God. Preachers, according to Chapter 17, are not to do so except according to "the rite and practice of the church" with the due permission of the minister (stipulations of Lateran IV are echoed here) but all brothers may preach "by their deeds." Two chapters later, as if to press the point of orthodoxy, brothers are enjoined to live and speak "as Catholics" and those who do not are to be "expelled from our brotherhood."

The penultimate chapter consists of a long exhortation combined with prayerful outbursts of adoration. Replete with both trinitarian and christological themes one hears the passion of Francis coming through the text:

> Wherever we are
> let nothing hinder us,
> nothing separate us,
> nothing come between us.
>
> Wherever we are,
> in every place
> at every hour
> at every time of day
> every day and continually,
> let all of us truly and humbly believe
> hold in our heart and love,
> honor, adore, and serve
> praise and bless,
> glorify and bless,

Magnify and give thanks
To the Most High and Supreme and Eternal God
Trinity and Unity. . . .

The next, and final chapter, has been the source of some
scholarly speculation about whether it belongs in this redac-
tion of the rule or not. It seems to convey the anxiety that Francis felt about the slippage of the ideals he held most dear about
the order of lesser brothers and, in that sense, echoes what
Francis wrote in his *Testament*. Chapter 24 insists that nothing
is to be deleted or added to what was written in this rule. The
penultimate sentence is starkly apodictic in tone: "The brothers may have no other rule."

In fact, the brothers would get another rule. The Rule of
1221 never got official approval. The reasons for its rejection are
not easy to understand but it is clear that as it stood the 1221
version, while zealous and redolent of holiness, was simply too
prolix to pass muster with the legal-minded Roman curia.
Lovers of precise legal language would have little patience with
the more homiletical portions of the rule. It was simply too
discursive; it cried out, in the eyes of the curial officials, for the
touch of the canon lawyer. Accordingly, the rule was rewritten
by Francis with the aid of some learned friars, probably at the
hermitage at Fonte Colombo outside Rieti. After discussion at
the June chapter of the lesser brothers, the new draft of the rule
was submitted to Rome in 1223. It was approved by Pope
Honorius III on November 29, 1223, and now stands as the
foundational document of the three orders of the Franciscan
family. Because it did get the papal seal it is now known as the
Regula Bullata.

A comparison between the two rules is instructive. Gone are the hortatory passages and the scriptural texts. The twenty-four chapters of the earlier rule are now reduced to twelve (alluding by symbolic number to the "apostolic" character of the rule?). Each chapter of the 1223 rule has a heading summarizing the content of that chapter. The twelve chapters may be summarized as following:

1. The rule and life of the lesser brothers is to observe the gospel by living in obedience, without possessions of one's own, and in chastity.
2. Prospective members are to be observant Catholics. Regulations concerning disposition of personal wealth, the proper clothing of postulants and professed members of the community, and simplicity of life are laid out.
3. Rules for liturgical prayer, fasting, and manner of going abroad in the world on mission.
4. The use of money prohibited.
5. Obligation to work but without cash wages.
6. Necessity of dispossession of goods; the begging of alms; the care of sick brethren.
7. Penance(s) for errant brothers.
8. Rules for electing the minister general; the Pentecost chapter.
9. Rules for preaching.
10. Admonition and correction of brothers.
11. Relationship with women and prohibition of entering convents.
12. Permission needed before going out to Saracens and other non-believers.

When comparing the two rules the differences are clear. Some specific regulations in the earlier rule (for example, prohibiting the use of horses; rules about the reception of the sacraments; etc.) are suppressed. Other chapters are radically shortened. The chapter on preaching in the earlier rule, with its long peroration and prayer, was reduced from over nineteen separate verses to barely ten lines. The prologue and first chapter of the earlier rule are collapsed in chapter one of the 1223 rule with the catena of scriptural texts excised. In short, the differences between the two rules is mainly (although not exclusively) an exercise of editing, pruning, and telescoping the text of the former into something that approached the canonical style of the latter. It is for scholars to debate the extent that Francis's intentions were compromised in the emendations made in 1223 but it is patent that the scriptural tone garnered from the old form of life orally approved by the pope more than a decade earlier disappeared in favor of a more precise legal statement.

The problem that arises from the legal stipulations of the Franciscan way of life is easy to state, namely, the near impossibility of capturing in legal terms the esprit of a movement that was based on the intuitions of a singular religious genius. Attempts to sort out the legal issues concerning the Franciscan way of life would vex the Franciscan family long after the death of Francis. That being said we should also note, from a human commonsense point of view, that the emergence of some kind of structure, fortified by a rule of life, had a certain inevitability to it. Free-floating movements without structure have an almost inevitable tendency either to peter out or turn into anarchic curiosities.

What one sees at close range with respect to the Franciscan *religio* is a microcosm of the larger problem within all institutional religion. One could say that the persistent problem of Catholicism has been to somehow balance fidelity to the gospel with the need for some kind of institutional coherence. The most fruitful way the problem has been handled, when recognized, has been to constantly refine the institutional weight of structures against the sources of the faith in an ongoing process of what the French call *ressourcement*. This demands a firm understanding that Christianity in general and any of its particular manifestations, such as religious movements, are not perfectionist sects but ongoing attempts to strive toward the demands of the gospel itself.

As far as we can tell, Francis tried very hard to do what he had originally set out to do: preach penance, live by the gospel demands, and, as occasion demanded, tend to the growth of the movement he had inspired. One thing is very clear: he did not act as the "head" of an order. There is no evidence that he stopped his wandering ways, his times of retreat, or his care for the immediate needs of the day. Indeed, while he was obedient to the letter, the adoption of the Rule of 1223 did very little to change his own way of life. His anxiety concerned those who would subvert that way of life for others. It seems clear that Francis held on to his way of life, and the Franciscan *religio* was taking on a life of its own as it grew. Even the charismatic power of Francis's life and witness could not change that.

After his return from the Middle East Francis traveled and preached in Italy until his worsening health made this impossible. The precise character of his itinerary is impossible to determine in detail. We know, for example, that he toured southern Italy in 1221 and 1222; we also hear of him preaching in Bologna. Those journeys were punctuated by moments of retreat into contemplative solitude, as was his custom from the beginning of his converted life.

Contemplative retreat was always part of Francis's life; it was something that he urged on his friars. After the death of Francis in 1226 the hermit impulse increased among some of the friars and some of them, in reaction to those who accented the preaching and academic life, turned their lives into almost continual contemplative retreat. For some generations after the death of Francis some of the friars, especially those in the Marches of Italy, were more contemplative than active in their style of life.

It was out of this esteemed practice that there grew another rule written by Francis, the Rule for Hermitages. When it was written, as with so many texts from Francis, is not clear. Editors place it sometime between 1217 and 1221. The text itself is brief, in modern translation barely a full printed page. The themes of going aside for contemplative prayer; the models of the Gospel figures of Martha and Mary who are emblematic of the active and contemplative life; and the provision for individual cells clustered near each other reflect long usages in the eremitical tradition. What is charming about this rule, however, is the language that Francis uses to describe the order of these contemplative retreats. He envisions a community of about four members, arranged among "mothers" who will see after the needs of the "sons" as well as provide an atmosphere of separation and silence for those who are to spend their time in prayer and meditation. This arrangement is seen as a reciprocal one. The rule concludes with these words: "The 'sons', however, may periodically assume the role of the 'mothers' taking turns for a time as they have mutually decided. . . ."

It is not possible to reconstruct fully what the actual setting of these retreats was like, but we do know of various places in central Italy which tradition demarcates as places of Franciscan retreat. Judging from the description given in the "Rule for Hermitages" the community was not unlike those clusters of monastics who live in a very small settlement that in the Orthodox monastic tradition is known as a *skete*, although the Franciscan model seems more temporary — a period of retirement away from the work of preaching and mendicancy. Today, the more assiduous pilgrims to Assisi make their way the four kilometers up Monte Subasio which takes them to the hermitage of the *Carceri* (literally: "prison cells") where contemporary Franciscans still live and pray in a small friary. There were a number of such places which Francis knew and loved in his own lifetime and which, even today, are marked by modest friaries and shrines.

Less than a month after Pope Honorius III put his seal on the revised rule of Saint Francis, the exhausted saint found himself in the town of Greccio just a few days before Christmas. It was a feast for which Francis had a special love. According to Thomas of Celano's second life of the saint, he observed the day "with inexpressible eagerness over all the other feasts, saying that it was the feast of feasts, on which God, having become a tiny infant, clung to human breasts." That insight of Francis about the helplessness of the Infant Christ is consistent with his more general understanding of the Incarnation and not unconnected to his love for and understanding of the hidden Christ in the eucharist. Francis never ceased to wonder at the implication of the simple phrase "The Word became flesh" (Jn 1:14). He saw in the Incarnation a humility in the Son of God that allowed him to be an infant, to put himself under the obedience of the Holy Family, and finally to die on the cross, naked and alone. If one is to understand such things as the emphasis of Francis on poverty one must keep in the background of such considerations his emphasis on the humility of Christ as part of the Incarnation itself.

According to Thomas of Celano he was so taken with the feast of Christmas that "He wanted the poor and hungry to be filled by the rich and oxen and asses to be spoiled with extra hay." "If ever I speak with the emperor," he would say, "I will beg him to issue a general decree that all who can should throw wheat and grain along the roads, so that on the day of such a great solemnity the birds may have an abundance, especially our sisters the larks."

Christ not only humbled himself by taking on flesh as an infant but he did so in the meanest of circumstances: in a manger at Bethlehem because "there was no room for them at the inn" (Lk 2:7). Francis was not insensitive to the fact that Mary and Joseph attended the birth of their child far from their home as part of a crowd who were, in effect, homeless. Sensitivity to such poverty may explain why Francis, some days before Christmas, contacted a local noble of Greccio named Giovanni whom Francis knew and admired because of his charity. He asked Giovanni to prepare a place for the celebration of the Christmas mass (it was actually Christmas Eve by our reckoning) in a poor stable with a manger and the traditional presence of the ox and the ass. Francis invited the lesser brothers who lived in the environs to come and light the place with their torches and lanterns for the celebration of mass.

Francis himself served as deacon at the Christmas mass and, as Thomas of Celano wrote in his first life of the saint, "with full voice sings the Gospel" and preaches with such love and tenderness that saying the word *Bethlehem* "he fills his whole mouth with sound but even more with sweet affection." He subtly alludes to a miraculous moment when Francis, according to those who were there, seems to hold the Christ Child in his arms during the homily. Saint Bonaventure, in his major life of the saint, fills out that story by making the witness to the event, the same Sir John (Giovanni) who "had abandoned military service for the love of Christ," claim that he saw a beautiful little boy asleep in the crib and that "the blessed Father Francis embraced it in both of his arms and seemed to wake it from sleep."

That first Christmas at Greccio captured the imagination of those who first heard of it. By the time Thomas of Celano wrote his first life (had he been at the original event in 1223?) he noted that there already was a chapel built over the site with an altar marking the place of the first Christmas mass. He also reported that some of the hay which had been used for the liturgy had been distributed to people who used it both to aid sick animals and some humans who had various illnesses. Therein marks the beginning of a highly complex Christmas custom whose final end is the beautiful custom of the Christmas creche.

Thomas of Celano's account of the Greccio Christmas marked the end of his first book of the life of Francis. It obviously represented a high point for him since, by the time

Thomas writes, there is already an established tradition of celebrating Christmas in this fashion, a tradition that is observed to this day in the Franciscan friary at Greccio. Scholars have maintained that the event at Greccio might have been the origin (or, more likely, the popularization) of the custom of building Christmas creches in Catholic churches to celebrate the nativity of Christ. Long before the time of Francis there had been a tradition of honoring the birth of Christ in various ways. As early as the late fifth century there was an oratory annexed to the basilica of Saint Mary Major in Rome built as a replica of the cave of Bethlehem. A century later the same Roman basilica claimed to have relics of the original crib. Depictions of the Christmas scene go back as early as late antique sculptured panels on Christian sarcophagi.

What was unique about Francis's notion was the use of live animals in an authentic setting of a stable. It was only in the seventeenth century that the Capuchins (a reform movement of the Franciscans so named because of the length of their hood — a *capuche* in Italian) encouraged the erection of Christmas crib scenes in private homes as a way of encouraging devotions to the humanity of Christ. The custom of erecting public creche scenes now is so common that one finds it not only in Catholic churches but among Protestant ones and as lawn decorations in front of homes. It may well be that the Franciscan tendency to create Christmas creches inspired music to be sung at Christmas like the lauds composed by the Franciscan Jacopone of Todi that developed into the traditional Christmas carol. Later, of course, would come the charming mystery plays that would celebrate the mystery of Christmas.

The intense focus on the humanity of Christ, manifested in this case in the nativity of Jesus, was not peculiar to the spirituality of Francis. There is a tradition that goes back at least as long as the prayers and meditations of Saint Anselm of Canterbury (died 1109), which dwells intensely on Jesus in his life and his passion. That form of devotion reached a new pitch with the intensely affective piety of the twelfth-century Cistercians. What Francis accomplished was to put into concrete visual terms the things that he read or heard in the Gospel. In that sense his spirituality was a kind of performance in which the gospel was a script that gave him directions not about how to think but about how to act. If the gospel said that the giving away of goods led to perfection, Francis took that as a stage direction. If Christ was born in a stable then surely when he was, as it were, re-born in the eucharistic liturgy then it was fitting to create that setting to remind us of poverty and humility.

The Franciscan emphasis on the concrete historicity of the gospel events had a profound impact on the spirituality of the Middle Ages as well as on the emerging realism of late medieval art. That the sixteenth-century *Spiritual Exercises* of Saint Ignatius of Loyola instructed those who meditate to create in their minds and imagination a "composition of place" — to picture the real setting of the Gospel events — has a lineage that runs back through Francis and earlier to the Cistercians and the piety of Anselm of Canterbury.

Francis most likely stayed in semi-retreat in Greccio through the Easter season. His exact itinerary through the summer months is not all that clear. What we do know is that he headed north and by the feast of the Assumption of Mary (August 15) he arrived at Mount LaVerna near Arezzo to begin a period of fasting and prayer on a mountain ceded for his use by a local noble. What happened in that retreat has almost become identified with who Francis was and what happened to him.

CHAPTER FIVE

The Stigmata of Saint Francis

With the gnarls of the nails in thee, niche of the lance, his Lovescape crucified and seal of his seraph-arrival!

Gerard Manley Hopkins
"The Wreck of the Deutschland"

IF ONE ACCEPTS as authentic (and there are those who have great doubts about it) the circular letter Brother Elias of Cortona sent to announce the death of Saint Francis, then it is in that letter that we first learn about the experience Saint Francis had on Mount LaVerna in October of 1224. In the course of his circular Elias wrote of a great joy to announce:

Not long before his death, our brother and father appeared crucified, bearing in his body the five wounds which are truly the marks of Christ. His hands and feet had, as it were, the openings of the nails and were pierced front and back revealing the scars and showing the nails' blackness. His side, moreover, seemed opened by a lance and often emitted blood.

79

St. Francis receiving the stigmata
The Master of St. Francis Cycle, Upper Church, Assisi

What Brother Elias (putatively) wrote was a description of the condition of the body of Saint Francis at the time of his death. He does not say how these marks were made, when they were made, or anything more specific than the fact that Francis bore these wounds on his body. If we turn to the earliest life of Francis by Thomas of Celano we get further information. Indeed, if the Elias letter does date to a later period, Celano provides the earliest information we possess, since his life was written in less than a decade after the saint's death.

According to Thomas of Celano signs of the nails began to appear on the body of Francis soon after an ecstatic visionary experience he had on LaVerna of a six-winged seraph (see Is 6:2) fixed to a cross. This event took place on September 14, which is the feast of the Exaltation of the Holy Cross, the traditional beginning of the autumn penitential season for vowed religious. The wounds were similar to those Francis saw on the crucified man hovering over him in the vision. Thomas describes the wounds in this fashion:

> His hands and feet seem to be pierced through the middle by nails, with the heads of the nails appearing on the inner part of his hands and on the upper part of his feet, and their points protruding on the opposite sides. These marks on the inside of his hands were round, but rather oblong on the outside; and small pieces of flesh were visible like the points of nails, bent over and flattened, extending beyond the flesh around them. On his feet, the mark of the nails were stamped in the same way and raised above the surrounding flesh. His right side was marked with an oblong scar, as if pierced with a lance,

and this often dripped blood, so that his tunic and under-garments were frequently stained with his holy blood.

Thomas went on to say that Francis almost never spoke of the phenomenon and that during the saint's life he concealed what had happened even from those who were his disciples. It is a commonplace of Franciscan scholarship to note that the event commonly called the "stigmata" of Saint Francis is treated diversely in the early sources. There is an apparent contrast between, say, the relatively brief account in the first life by Thomas of Celano and the more dense (and more overtly theological) rendering found in the thirteenth chapter of the major life by Saint Bonaventure. We also possess, written in his own hand, a brief resume by Brother Leo, inscribed on the side of an autograph blessing of Francis that the saint wrote for Leo, who was one of his companions at LaVerna. That blessing will be discussed later in this chapter. The pertinent words of Leo are, "After the vision and message of the Seraph and the impression of Christ's stigmata upon his body, he composed these praises. . . ." This annotation, of course, was written some time after the actual events on LaVerna.

This extraordinary phenomenon of the stigmata, the subject of much scholarly attention, raises a series of questions that admit of no easy answer. We should note, as a preliminary point, that the fact of the stigmata (that is, visible wounds on a person's body) is not in any sense *ex professo* a miraculous event; it could be only a psychosomatic reaction to intense emotional experience. The Catholic church has never defined the stigmata of Francis as something purely miraculous and, indeed, more generally, has been slow to pronounce in favor of the many claims of stigmatization either in the contemporary world (such as the recently canonized Padre Pio) or in the historical past. Claims of the stigmata in the history of the church all postdate the experience of Saint Francis with many instances alleged in modern times. These claims are received by church authority with extreme caution and not a little skepticism.

The interventions of church authority in the time of Francis apropos the question of the stigmata of Saint Francis dealt only with the historical issue: did Francis experience the stigmata? Three popes (Gregory IX, Alexander IV, and Nicholas III) between 1237 and 1291 defended the historicity of the stigmata in reaction to widespread doubts originating among those ill-disposed toward the Franciscans, even though the stigmata was not mentioned in the bull of canonization in 1228. The sermons preached by Saint Bonaventure for the feast of Saint Francis in the late 1250s and 1260s take great pains to argue for the truth about the stigmata and, in that emphasis, seem to indicate that many were dubious about it. Bonaventure was, after all, an able apologist against those who were vociferous critics of the Franciscans in general.

In 1924, as part of the celebration honoring the seven hundredth anniversary of the stigmatization, Pope Pius XI accepted as authentic the historic record of the event but was careful not to ascribe it to divine intervention. A feast honoring the imposition of the stigmata on Francis is observed in the Franciscan sanctoral cycle which gives some liturgical support for the historical claim. That feast (on September 17) goes back to the early fourteenth century and may well have been established to give liturgical strength to the Franciscan claims about

the stigmata of the saint against its doubters. The feast was observed for a period in the sanctoral cycle of the universal Roman calendar for periods of time but is not observed today.
The Roman martyrology (revised in 2001) has a biographical
statement for the feast day (October 4) of the saint but does
not mention the stigmata.

About the phenomenon of the stigmata, we should note the
following. First, there is no clear consensus about the nature of
the wounds that Francis bore. Elias described them as punc-
ture wounds or holes in his hands. Thomas of Celano, by contrast, describes them as looking like protuberances as if they
were nails with the heads in the palms and raised indentations
like points on the backs of the hands. He also said that the
wound in the side of Francis actually bled on a regular basis. In
a sense, the description by Elias posits a source of the wounds
as coming from outside Francis (from the vision of the Seraph?) while Thomas of Celano seems to indicate that the
wounds appeared from within Francis. Both accounts, of
course, equate the phenomenon with the intense single-
minded attempt of Francis to live as closely to the model of
Christ crucified as possible. Since it is quite possible that both
men actually saw the body of the dead Francis it is not clear
how to resolve what appears to be contrary accounts of what
the wounds looked like. One contemporary scholar (Chiara
Frugoni) thinks that what Thomas of Celano saw were ulcer-
ated protuberances caused, perhaps, by leprosy or something
similar contracted during his ministrations to the poor of Italy.
There is no way to know for sure.

Second, whatever we are to make about the complex tradition of the stigmata itself and whether there were earlier exam-

ples of it in medieval spiritual literature is a subject best reserved for the scholars. We do know that before the time of Francis certain medieval mystics inflicted wounds on themselves in imitation of Christ's passion, but no scholar has suggested that Francis did that. Nor is it clear, if, in fact, it is true, that a similar phenomenon among Shi'ite mystics in Islam who exhibited the "wounds of Ali" did so prior to Francis or at all — or even in imitation of the purported stigmata of Francis about which they may have heard.

What is clear is that the event of LaVerna became *the* example of the stigmata in the subsequent tradition and, as such, is always identified with the saint. Furthermore, the very novelty of the idea inflamed the imagination of the Christian world of the West. One can walk into any museum that holds those great Italo-Byzantine crucifixes so characteristic of the period and almost infallibly date them from the second half of the thirteenth century, that is, after the death of Francis, if they focus heavily on depicting the wounds of Christ. The rise of such popular devotions upon the wounds of Christ or the pierced body of Christ testifies to the power of the story of the stigmata. Writing nearly a century after the event, Dante, in the *Paradiso,* says that on the crag between the Tiber and the Arno (that is, LaVerna) Francis, in "tears and joy," "took Christ's final seal, the holy wounds which he bore two years" (xi:107-108).

One cannot read of this great encounter in the life of Saint Francis without thinking back to an autobiographical cry of the apostle Paul writing to the churches of Galatia: "From now on, let no one make trouble for me; for I carry the marks (Greek: *stigmata*) of Jesus on my body" (Gal 6:17). The Pauline emphasis of identification with Christ as well as the gospel theme of the following of Christ is evident in the life of Francis through his desire to follow the poverty of Christ from his poor birth in a stable through his desolation on the cross. It should not be thought odd that the space between the celebration of the Christmas liturgy in Greccio and the experience that Francis had on LaVerna was a period of only about nine months. To separate the celebration of the nativity from the terrible experience on LaVerna would be to give in to the temptation to sentimentalize the Christmas religious experience of Francis.

In a sense those two moments at Greccio and La Verna were two parentheses that summed up the evangelical vision of Francis. If the later Franciscans were to enter into sterile debates about the meaning of poverty, that all too human fact stands in contrast to how Francis saw poverty: as a self-emptying whose meaning had to be anchored in the reality of the gospel message whose center is the cross. That self-emptying began, of course, when the Word became flesh, when the Son of God was born of Mary in a simple stable in Bethlehem. The seal of the stigmata is crucial as a counterweight to any attempt to romanticize Francis as a medieval doctor Doolittle who innocently hymned the cosmos and its inhabitants in a constant state of felicity.

In fact, the Franciscans of the next generation turned the event of the stigmata into a vehicle for profound mystical meditation. Saint Bonaventure's classic spiritual treatise, *The Soul's Journey to God*, is set within the context of the stigmata. Bonaventure tells us that he wrote his treatise while on retreat at LaVerna under the inspiration of "the miracle that had occurred to blessed Francis in this very place, the vision of the six-winged seraph in the form of the Crucified."

The claims about the stigmata of Saint Francis did more than provide a source for literary tropes for the spiritual literature of the Middle Ages. It provided tacit approval for all kinds of ascetic practices in honor of the passion of Christ many of which would find their way into the iconography of Christian art. It also gave warrant to those who yearned for, made claims about, or experienced the wounds of Christ as a result of their own intense religious experiences. Some saints wrote about intense wounds they bore internally with no external manifestation (the invisible stigmata of Saint Catherine of Siena and Saint Teresa of Avila) while others in the subsequent history of the church are reported to have external signs. The officials of the Catholic church have been extremely reluctant to judge such claims as supernatural. As early as the seventeenth century great spiritual masters like Saint Francis de Sales have judged such phenomena as more likely coming from intense spiritual experiences.

We have already noted that during their retreat at LaVerna Francis wrote out a blessing for his old companion, Brother Leo. That autograph, one of two that we have from the saint's own hand, contains a blessing that Francis composed for Leo.

On one side of the page Brother Leo wrote that on the other side were praises composed by Saint Francis who "wrote them in his own hand, thanking God for the kindness bestowed on him." On the other side Leo repeats "In a similar way he made with his own hand this sign TAU together with a skull." The actual page is not in good shape with certain illegibilities caused by creases and wear at the edges of the page. The "Praises of God" is a pastiche made up of fragments from the psalms and certain passages from the New Testament. These are the concluding lines:

> You are beauty. You are meekness.
> You are the protector, You are our custodian and defender.
> You are our strength. You are our refreshment.
>   You are our hope.
> You are our sweetness. You are our eternal life:
> Great and wonderful Lord, Almighty God, Merciful savior.

The page ends with a blessing for Brother Leo with the conclusion drawn from the Book of Numbers (6:24-27): "May he turn his countenance to you and give you peace. May the Lord bless you, Brother Leo."

Among the authentic writings of Saint Francis we have some other prayers in the form of salutations composed either from traditional titles in the case of his salutation of the Blessed Virgin Mary or his salutation of the holy virtues. What these various prayers have in common is that they are written in strophes of simple pithy lines. Here is an example from the one on the Blessed Virgin:

> Hail his palace!
> Hail his tabernacle!
> Hail his dwelling!
> Hail his robe!
> Hail his servant!
> Hail his mother!

And the opening of the salutation of the virtues:

Hail, Queen Wisdom!
May the Lord protect you!
With your sister, holy pure simplicity!
Lady holy Poverty,
May the Lord protect you
with your sister, holy humility.
Lady Holy Charity,
may the Lord protect you
with your sister, holy obedience. . . .

It is not clear when Francis wrote any of these prayers (or his wonderful paraphrase of the Lord's Prayer) with the exception of the Blessing for Brother Leo, which is datable to 1224. Nor are we clear, again with the exception of the Brother Leo text, for whom these prayers were intended or toward what end. It would be a safe guess, however, to think that they were composed for his brothers or for his lay followers. The fact that they are done in simple strophic fashion, redolent with fragments from the scriptures, would lead us to think that they were meant to be easily memorized either for personal devotion or for proclamation when the friars preached. Since books were at a premium and illiteracy high, they were most likely intended to increase the spiritual inventory of those who were committed to the life of prayer and the work of preaching and teaching. Given Francis's predilection for the troubadour tradition it is quite possible that they were also set to music and sung, since we know from the sources that Francis loved to sing as he traveled in the company of his friars.

What is the meaning of the mark of the TAU to which Leo alludes in his notation on the blessing manuscript? The Greek letter Tau is similar to our capital letter "T." Saint Bonaventure, borrowing from Thomas of Celano's second life, said that Francis "venerated this symbol with great affection, often spoke highly of it, and signed it with his own hand at the end of every letter he sent. . . ." Francis evidently got the idea of using this symbol after Pope Innocent III preached a sermon to open the Fourth Lateran Council on the text from the prophet Ezekiel: "Go through the city, through Jerusalem, and put a mark on the foreheads of those who sigh and groan over all the abominations that are committed in it" (9:4).

Bonaventure, in his prologue to the major life said that Francis signed his followers "with the cross of penance and clothing them with his habit, which is in the form of a cross." Since the early sources also say that Francis chalked a cross on the clothes he adopted when he returned his finery to his father before Bishop Guido it may well be that Francis saw his new life as an analogue to the crusaders who "took up the cross" to do battle against the Muslims in the Holy Land. Many contemporary Franciscans and those influenced by Franciscan spirituality have adopted a simple wooden TAU cross in honor of the veneration Francis showed toward that symbol he so loved.

Francis reflected his devotion toward the passion of Christ by composing a little office of prayers (composed of lines from the Psalms) that he and his companions would recite from Holy Thursday evening through the vigil for Easter. These prayers were adjunct to the normal recitation of the office for this period and may well have developed into a kind of private prayer that was used beyond the triduum of Holy Week. Commentators on these Psalm pastiches attempt to show that Francis chose his lines from scripture to honor actual moments of the unfolding passion of Jesus. Thus, for example, the hour of Terce has lines of mockery for it was then, it was thought, that Jesus was scourged; at Sext, lines reflected the actual crucifixion, and so on. The point of such exercises was, of course, to enter into the passion of Christ in some performative fashion — to "dramatize" the passion just as Francis wishes to dramatize the nativity by the setting he chose for the midnight mass at Greccio.

It is not too fanciful to see the Passion Office that Francis wrote as a distant ancestor of those forms of devotion, developed largely by Franciscans, that acted out the events of the life and acts of Jesus. While the fourteen stations of the cross, found in almost all Catholic churches, were stabilized only in the eighteenth century by the Franciscan preacher Leonard of Saint Maurice, the devotional practice goes back to the late middle ages, encouraged by the Franciscans who developed the practice from the even earlier pilgrimage routes of the visitors to Jerusalem who visited in order sites designated as places where Christ was present during his passion. The traditional prayer used in making the stations today ("We adore you O Christ, and we bless you because by your holy cross you have redeemed the world") is a variation of a prayer that Francis himself composed and cites in his *Testament* saying that he "would pray with simplicity in this fashion."

CHAPTER SIX

Saint Francis and the Love of Creation

Let everything that has breath praise the Lord!

Psalm 150:6

IF OUR CONTEMPORARIES know anything about Saint Francis it is that he loved animals. He has been adopted by the ecological movement as its patron saint. Many places honor his memory by having animals brought to church to have them blessed on his feast day, October 4. He has been called the "saint of nature" even though he never used the word "nature," and if he heard the word would have recognized it as meaning something quite different from what we mean today. Nonetheless, it is true that Francis did love animals and, further, the beauties of the natural world like the sun, moon, stars, and flowers and fruits of Mother Earth. And it is also true that the earliest stories about him note this fact at some length. In fact, on the wall opposite from where these lines are being written, there is an icon of Francis gently shaking the paw of the wolf of Gubbio; to that incident we shall return. Francis applied in his life that frequent theme in the

Psalms of David that all creation should (and does) praise the Lord.

Elsewhere I have already raised cautions against sentimentalizing the story of Francis. There is a particular danger in isolating Francis's love for the created world from his larger understanding about the Christian faith. That tendency to romanticize has its roots in the romantic rediscovery of the saint in the nineteenth century and continues to this day. The correct way to put the issue of Francis and the world of nature into some kind of balance is to understand the context of his own time, the broader context of Christian hagiography generally, and the theological presuppositions of his biographers. Such contextualization helps us to understand Francis without any denigration of his profound simplicity and his overwhelming sense of love and awe for the created order. Nor should it escape our attention that Francis's great love for creation was a direct rebuke to the then powerful Cathars who denigrated the world of matter as sinful and something from which to escape. In that sense, Francis's love for the natural created world had a polemical edge to it. It was a way of disconfirming some of the pessimistic teachings of the Cathars. While Francis had a healthy respect for the practice of traditional asceticism, he never denigrated the material world; he did not see the gift of creation in any way but gift. He certainly never saw material creation as evil. In that sense — and there is a paradox here — the love that Francis showed for all of creation was an act of resistance against those who would totally "spiritualize" faith.

All of the early biographers mention his love for animals, they recount his preaching to the birds (that incident occurs in some of the earliest visual tributes to the saint like the

Berlingheri altarpiece at Pescia), and they note his simple joy in the beauty of the created order. The twenty-first chapter of Celano's first life of the saint narrates his preaching to the birds and then goes on to say from then on "he carefully exhorted all birds, all animals, all reptiles, and also insensible creatures to praise and love the Creator, because, daily invoking the name of the Savior, he observed their obedience in his own experience."

The first thing to note about that passage is that Francis "observed their obedience." What does that mean? It does not mean that Francis anthropomorphized the animal and sensate world. What is behind the sentiment expressed by Celano was the root theological conviction, expressed in a more scholarly fashion by the scholastic doctors, that everything in creation is not only good (as the opening chapter of Genesis states emphatically) but also praises God by its very existence. Furthermore, the manner of praise coming from creation derives from the very teleology of their existence: fish praise God by swimming in the sea as birds do by flying in the air. Behind that conviction is not only Aristotle's notion of final causality (that everything has a finality: a rock is meant to be a rock) but the sense that one finds in the scriptures that everything in the world obeys the creative intent of God and manifests the creative wisdom of God. Francis knew by instinctive faith what the psalmist proclaimed: "The heavens proclaim the glory of God/The sky proclaims its builder's craft./One day to the next conveys that message;/one night to the next imparts that knowledge" (Ps 19:1-2). In the generations after Saint Francis, Saint Thomas Aquinas and Saint Bonaventure would put this ancient truth into formal theological language. "Whoever is not enlightened by such splendor of creation things is blind/ whoever is not awakened by such outcries is deaf/whoever does not praise God because of all these effects is dumb/Whoever does not discover the First Principle from such clear signs, is a fool" — thus Bonaventure in *The Soul's Journey to God* after he describes the footprints of God in the created order.

It is not incidental that Francis exhorts creatures to "praise and love their Creator" since the love that Francis expresses for the world roots itself in a deep theology of creation. The created world is, as it were, a sacrament of the free gift of creation coming from the hand of God: "Ever since the creation of the world God's eternal power and divine nature, invisible though they are, have been understood and seen through the things God has made" (Rom 1:20). When Francis exhorts created beings to give praise to God he enters into their praise as a free and responsive person who praises God by the gratitude he has for that free gift of creation. Saint Bonaventure makes that precise point about Saint Francis when he notes, in his major life of the saint, that "when he considered the primordial source of all things, he was filled with abundant piety, calling creatures, no matter how small, by the name of brother and sister, because he knew that they had the same source as himself." Francis also knew that the creative word uttered by God was the Word of God who held all things in his hand (Jn 1:1-3).

However beautiful and various the created world may be, it is also, as Tennyson wrote famously, "red in tooth and claw." Which brings us to the matter of wolves. According to several sources, Francis helped the peasants of Greccio protect themselves from the ravening wolves who attacked both man and beast in winter by taming the wolves. The most famous story of wolves in relation to Saint Francis is the charming tale re-counted in the *Little Flowers of Saint Francis* about the wolf of Gubbio. Gubbio is a small Umbrian town northeast of Assisi where Francis stayed early in his wanderings. According to the story, a ferocious wolf attacked both people and beasts in the Umbrian town of Gubbio. Francis went outside the town, spoke to the wolf who agreed to stop his attacks (Francis shook his paw as a sign of assent) for which, in turn, the people of the town would provide food for the wolf. Brother Wolf observed his part of the bargain for two years; when he died, the towns-people buried him, and according to the guidebooks his burial place is marked to this day at a church aptly named "della pace" ("of peace").

That story may have a historical core with the wolf being, in fact, a pitiless ruler who terrorized the citizenry by his rapa-cious demands and depredations. A medieval commentator on the story said that the wolf was a symbol of the Italian people! Saint Francis, who made a vocation out of pacification, may have reformed a bellicose warlord. Whatever the origin of the story, there is a fundamental and theological motif within it. After all, the prophet Isaiah proclaimed that the coming mes-siah would inaugurate a time when the wolf would lie down with the lamb in a peaceful kingdom. The story might well il-lustrate the common perception that Francis was another Christ — an *alter christus*. In other words, behind the charm-ing folktale recorded in the *Fioretti* may well be a complex theological observation about Francis as an imitator of Christ and Francis as a preacher of peace and reconciliation.

There is more. According to the biblical tradition, in the pe-riod before the Fall, the animals were in harmony with human beings — Adam, according to Genesis, naming the animals. It was only through sin, according to tradition, that this harmony was interrupted. To return to an Edenic simplicity through the cultivation of virtue and the erasure of vice was the mark of those saints who had achieved purity of heart. The ability of Francis to live in peace with the animal world, then, was a sign of his purity and holiness. The stories about his rescue of lambs, the tame pheasant given to him by a nobleman of Siena, the cricket that would perch on his shoulder, the birds who would listen attentively to him as he preached, and the other stories that make the early legends so charming have behind them a theological perception about the state of the soul of Francis.

This Edenic harmony between a sainted figure and the animal world is not peculiar to Saint Francis. Students of hagiography can point to many similar stories told of hermits, monks, and others who lived in harmony with animals as a sign of their recovery of a state of innocence. Celtic hagiography is replete with such instances (as well as a literature of prayers exemplifying the presence of God in the beauty of creation). There is a particularly charming story told of the sixth-century Irish bishop Saint Colman who, according to the legend, would be awakened by a cock each morning for his Vigils; a mouse would scurry about him to keep him from falling asleep at his prayers; and a fly would mark the spot on his psalter he was to read from that day.

Such examples are not restricted to that Celtic strain of Christian spirituality. A few examples, all taken from the calendar of saints for March 5, might make the case. Saint Mark the Hermit (circa 400) healed and tamed a hyena and her whelp.

Saint Gerasimus (died 475) had a lion who was so faithful a companion that it stretched itself out on the saint's tomb and died of grief. The fifth-century abbot and bishop, Saint Cioran, had a whole menagerie of friendly animals around his cell: Brothers Boar, Badger, Fox, Wolf, and Deer. When Brother Fox ate the hermit's sandals out of sheer hunger, the poor animal was put on a three-day fast for penance! All of these stories implicitly link the sanctity of the man of God with a return to the prelapsarian state of innocence and walking with God.

Curiously enough, this harmony with the animal world is not unconnected with the frequency with which Francis is described as stripping himself naked: before bishop Guido, on a preaching tour through a town as a symbol of his humility, or asking to be stripped naked and put on the bare soil at the time of his death. Francis, like Adam, was naked and not ashamed. Already in the early legends this penchant for nakedness is linked explicitly to three biblical themes: the command of God to Isaiah that the prophet preach naked and unshod; the nakedness of Christ when he was crucified ("nakedly following the naked Christ"); and the nakedness of Adam in the garden. Henri of Avanches makes the latter point explicitly when commenting on the incident of Francis naked before the bishop of Assisi. His versified life says that Francis was "like Adam" who was unashamed of his nakedness because of the purity of his soul.

The biblical background of Francis's love for the created world and its creatures was certainly in the mind of his earliest commentators as they reflected on the deeds of Francis. There is, however, one piece of evidence that comes directly from the saint about how he viewed the created world — his famous

"Canticle of Brother Sun." The canticle is recognized as one of the earliest poems written in the vernacular Italian. Written and expanded over the last years of the saint's life it may well have been composed by Francis to give the friars something to sing in the public squares of Italy when on their preaching missions.

Below is a free translation of my own with the added verses indicated either in *italics* or **bold**:

Most high, omnipotent, good Lord
To you alone belongs praise and glory,
Honor and blessing.
No one is worthy to breathe your name.
Be praised, my Lord, for all your creatures.
In the first place for [per] the blessed Brother Sun
who gives us the day and enlightens us through You.
He is beautiful and radiant in his great splendor
Giving witness to You, most omnipotent One.
Be praised, my Lord, for Sister Moon and the stars
Formed by You so bright, precious, and beautiful.
Be praised, My Lord, for Brother Wind
and the airy skies so cloudy and serene.
For every weather, be praised because it is life giving.
Be praised, My Lord, for Sister Water
so necessary yet humble, precious, and chaste.
Be praised, my Lord, for Brother Fire
who lights up the night.
He is beautiful and carefree, robust and fierce.
Be praised, my Lord, for our sister, Mother Earth
who nourishes and watches over us

while bringing forth abundant fruits and colored
 flowers and herbs.
*Be praised, my Lord, for those who pardon through Your love
and bear witness and trial.*
Blessed are those who endure in peace
for they will be crowned by You, Most High.
Be praised, my Lord, for our sister, bodily death.
Whom no one living can escape.
Woe to those who die in sin.
Blessed are those who discover Thy holy will.
The second death will do them no harm.
Praise and bless the Lord.
Render Him thanks.
Serve Him with great humility.
Amen.

According to the Assisi compilation (#84) Francis had the italicized verses added to the Canticle and then instructed the entire Canticle to be sung in the presence of the bishop and the mayor *(podestá),* which triggered a moment of religious zeal in both the authorities so that with "great kindness and love they embraced and kissed each other." While the incident may seem charming to us, in reality, given the place of honor in that society, it was a truly humble and uncharacteristic moment for both powerful men. The italicized lines were Francis's way of healing a civic rift between the mayor and the bishop.

The next section (#85) then tells us how Francis in this same period wrote some verses for the consolation of Saint Clare and the Poor Ladies who lived with her at San Damiano because of their distress at his poor health. Those verses, composed in the Umbrian dialect of Italian like the "Canticle," are dedicated to the sisters with the hope that they will persevere in their chosen life. They read:

> Listen, little poor ones, called by the Lord,
> Who have come together from many parts and provinces.
> Live always in truth that you may die in obedience.
> Do not look at life outside for that of the Spirit is better.
> I beg you through great love to use with discretion
> the alms which the Lord has given you.
> Those who are burdened with illness and others
>   who are wearied because of them,
> All of you: bear it in peace.
> For you will feel this fatigue for a very high price
> And each will be crowned queen in heaven with the
>   Virgin Mary.

Francis also added some final verses about death to his Canticle in his final days of suffering. They appear in the above translation in bold letters and will be taken up later in this volume.

There is a historic translation crux connected with the Canticle. The crux is such that the Canticle can mean one of several things depending on how one translates one small word. Saint Francis uses the preposition *per* which, as it stands in this poem, can actually have a number of quite different meanings. Does it mean "for" (as this translation gives it) in the sense of thanksgiving for the gifts of God? Does it mean "by" indicating that the sun and the other elements are instruments which give praise to God? Does it mean "through" which also indicates instrumentality but also the deeper sense of indicating the presence of God in all of creation as Saint Bonaventure would teach some decades later? Recent scholars have conceded that any of those renderings is legitimate from a theological point of view and could find arguments in medieval piety and theology to defend a given translation. This study, using the privilege of choice, has settled on "for" because of the profound sense of gratitude that shines through the life of Francis — although others take a quite different approach. While my translation emphasizes the spirit of gratitude that permeates the life of Francis, consideration will also be given to Francis's idea that all of creation speaks, in its own way, of God in general and the hidden presence of Christ the Word, through whom the world was created, in particular.

Originally, the Canticle ended with the strophes praising Mother Earth. Francis added the verses about peace and forgiveness when he mediated an episode of civil strife that agitated the civil and religious authorities of Assisi. The last lines, on sister death (in bold), were added later as Francis, who was dying in Assisi, greeted his own end not as an inexorable fate but as a welcoming presence. We are not certain how the verses for Clare and her sisters fit the canticle but they are written in the same dialect and seem to come from the same period.

Clearly the Canticle has antecedents in sacred scripture. The psalms, of course, come immediately to mind. Psalm 19 begins with the assertion that the heavens "tell" the glory of God and the firmament above "proclaims" God's handiwork. In the same psalm the rising of the sun is compared to a bridegroom coming from the marriage canopy. Psalm 104, a poetic retelling of the creation account of the opening chapter of the

Book of Genesis, is replete with images taken from the created world and its seasons. In places the psalms rise to ecstatic outbursts of praise: "O Lord, how manifold are your works! In wisdom You made them all; the earth is full of your creatures!" (v. 24). The psalm comes to a thunderous crescendo: "Praise the Lord, O my soul. Praise the Lord!" (v. 35) Finally, one hears the echo of Psalms 147, 148, and 150. Psalm 148 is most pertinent since the psalmist calls on both animate and inanimate creatures to praise God. Psalm 148 is a kind of cosmic praise in which both the macro world (heavens above the heavens) and the micro world (creeping things and flying birds) hymn God's glory.

The canticle of Saint Francis also has clear echoes of the so-called "Canticle of the Three Young Men" found in the Book of Daniel (3:52-90). This long hymn of praise was a standard feature of Sunday lauds in the liturgical office. It is fruitful to read the canticle in Daniel against the canticle of Saint Francis because the biblical canticle does call on the elements to praise God (as in verses 57-81) as if the entire creation were a kind of symphony of praise; thus giving the hymn a sense of instrumentality, which is how some read the canticle of Saint Francis. God is also blessed by the very presence of creation and its parts in the opening verses of the biblical canticle (verses 53-56). Finally, the biblical canticle, in the final verses, calls on us, echoing a line from the psalms, to give "thanks to the Lord for He is good" thus, finishing the great hymn with an expression of gratitude and adoration: "All who worship the Lord, bless the God of gods/sing praise to Him and give thanks to Him" (3:90). In short, when one parses the canticle in Daniel one finds a complex skein of sentiments that is captured so well in the layered meaning of the preposition *per* in the Italian text of Francis's beautiful hymn.

The early biographers of Francis paid explicit attention to his love for the created world and read various messages into that love. Thomas of Celano, after describing Francis preaching to the birds (a scene much loved in early Franciscan art), had Francis chiding himself for not doing so more frequently and then added: "From that day on he carefully exhorted all birds, all animals, all reptiles, and also insensible creatures to praise and love the Creator, because daily, invoking the name of the Savior, he observed their obedience in his own experience." By "obedience" Thomas of Celano refers to the well-known theological truth that all creatures give praise to God by being what they are created for; their very teleology orients them to God; humans, with their free will, are the only creatures who can thwart their (super)natural end, which is to be turned towards God.

In chapter 104 of his Second Life of the saint, Celano returns to a consideration of Francis's love for inanimate and animate creatures. Celano said that in the beauty of created things he saw Beauty itself. He remembered that Francis told the brother gardener to leave the edges of the garden untilled so that wild herbs and flowers may, in their season, "proclaim the Father of us all." He removed worms from pathways so that they would not be crushed and set out wine and honey for the bees so that they would not perish in the winter. A dubiously authentic letter of Francis has him instructing rulers to put out extra seed at Christmastime for the birds. Thomas of Celano, in a text we cited earlier, does say that Francis wanted to tell the emperor to give extra rations for birds on Christmas Day.

Thomas follows that introductory chapter up with a series of vignettes that has done much to crystallize the romantic picture of Francis we have inherited today. A little bird nestles in his hands; a falcon becomes domesticated at one of his hermitages; the bees provide honey for his drinking cup; he domesticates a pheasant that was sent to him for food; he bids "sister cricket" to sing praises to God, which the cricket did as Francis joined its music by singing along himself. The stories have the aura of the "peaceable kingdom" about them.

All of those vignettes (parallels may be found in Celtic hagiography) that seem so "sweet" to us had far more serious points to make for those who first heard them. They indicated that the created world was a good world and, in that affirmation, made a polemical point against the pessimism expressed by the heretical Cathars who saw the material universe as evil. They underscored Francis's idea (systematized later by figures like Saint Bonaventure) that the created world exemplifies and reveals the creative presence of God in the world. His love for animate and inanimate creation was fully in line with the biblical idea that the world was created through the Word (who was made flesh). And looking for the traces of God in the natural world was a way of contacting the cosmic Christ through whom the world was made.

One cannot leave this topic without pointing out what has been noted by scholars since the nineteenth century. The reputation of Francis was such that his emphasis on the beauty of creation in all of its manifestations turned the eyes of people toward this world with new appreciation for its beauty. Was it coincidental that after the death of Francis one sees a shift in Italian art from the somewhat static and hieratic forms of

Italo-Byzantine depictions to a more naturalistic setting for painting? Is there a nexus between not only a more observant depiction of natural settings in panel painting and fresco but also a more intense interest in representations of the nativity of Christ (as a consequence of the Greccio celebration of Christmas in a stable setting) and the human sufferings of Christ in depictions of the crucifixion? It would be difficult to make the shift consequent on the worldview of Francis in some kind of empirical way, but the possible influence of Francis and his followers has been explored since the nineteenth century. Thus, many writers have seen a link between Franciscan incarnationalism and its attendant exemplarism (the created world as a source for realizing the divine) and the shift to Renaissance realism in art.

Henry Thode's *Franz von Assisi und die Anfange der Kunst in Italien,* published in Berlin in 1885, made the argument, as the title of his book indicates, that one must look back to Francis in order to understand the origins of the Renaissance art movement. In a sense, Thode's book was a correction of the highly influential thesis of Walter Burckhardt's *The Civilization of the Renaissance in Italy* (1860), which argued that the Renaissance sprung forth, almost like a flower in the desert, from the wasteland of the Middle Ages. Thode argued (as would others after him) that the roots of the Renaissance were in the Middle Ages in general and in movements like that initiated by Francis in particular. Such an argument may be a commonplace today but it wasn't in the nineteenth century when everything medieval, in the eyes of many, was summed up in the phrase "Dark Ages." Thode and others like him may have viewed Francis romantically but there is no doubt that they did have an insight:

Francis had provided a fresh eye through which to explore the world.

If Francis and Franciscanism did impact the Renaissance imagination in some substantive fashion it certainly did not happen overnight. Nearly four generations, for example, separate Francis and Giotto's mature work. In between the two is still a body of rather conservative paintings. What seems safe to say, however, is that the Franciscan emphasis on the humanity of Christ in its preaching and the warrant allowed by the life of Francis to emphasize the corporeal did resonate broadly in the culture of the late twelfth and thirteenth centuries. It is not accidental that Italy, redolent of the saint's memory and example, broke with the Italo-Byzantine and International gothic styles of painting first.

Both the mendicant movement in general and the Franciscan movement in particular seemed like something new. It is not surprising, after all, that Dante would hail that "newness" in the *Paradiso* where he would devote not one but two cantos to hymn the work of Saint Dominic, founder of the Order of Preachers (the Dominicans), and Saint Francis while warning that their original fervor was already subject to decline. Dante knew firsthand about both of these movements since he had studied theology at the studium of the Dominicans at Santa Maria Novella in Florence and, across the city, had (perhaps?) entertained the idea of joining the Franciscans at their church of Santa Croce where Giotto had painted a spectacular fresco cycle on the life of Francis. The imprint of both Dominican and Franciscan thought is patent throughout Dante's *Commedia*.

CHAPTER SEVEN

The Final Years

When evening comes, you will be examined in love.

Saint John of the Cross

IN 1224 SAINT FRANCIS had been in retreat on the mountain of La Verna from the feast of the Assumption of Mary (August 15) to Saint Michael's Day, which falls on September 29. On or around the feast of the Exaltation (or Triumph) of the Holy Cross (September 14) is when Francis had the experience of what we now call the stigmata. September 14 is an important day in the life of vowed religious. It is the day that marks the beginning of the season of abstinence and fasting for monks and nuns as an observant anticipation of the joyous days of the Christmas season. The liturgical office of that day is replete with the imagery of the cross and the other elements attendant upon it. The experience of the stigmata cannot be seen apart from the emphases that fill the liturgical offices of that day.

After his retreat on La Verna Francis returned to the Portiuncula below the town of Assisi via towns that still are redolent with the memory of the saint: Borgo San Sepolcro,

Monte Casale, and Città di Castello. By December of that year, Francis undertook another preaching mission in his native Umbria and further north into the Marches of Italy. On that tour, he rode on a donkey — a sign that his health was in decline since he usually traveled on foot. His rule forbade the riding of horses since they were a "luxury" beyond what he allowed for his "Poor Brothers." In his major life of Francis Bonaventure says that he was carried "half dead" through the towns and villages because the pain in his feet from the stigmata did not allow him to walk. Of course, he was also in shockingly bad health in general since, as Bonaventure says, he treated his body as an overworked slave.

In the early spring (sometime in March?) Francis was back in Assisi where he visited Saint Clare at the convent of San Damiano. His eye illness had become much worse, so he stayed for a bit in a small cell near the quarters of the convent chaplain. The quarters must have been rather squalid since the sources tell us that Francis had trouble sleeping both because of the pain in his eyes and because his sleep was interrupted by mice that scurried about the little cell all night long. At the urging of Brother Elias, now the minister general of the Order, he consented to some medical treatment for his increasing blindness, but the treatment was deferred until the weather got warmer.

Scholars have speculated about the physical condition of Francis but have reached no consensus: did he have some form of tuberculosis of the bone? Leprosy? Was his illness of the eyes chronic conjunctivitis? No one knows. One thing is certain: any "medical" treatment given in his day was at best useless and quite likely dangerous. In fact, what we know about what was done to him that year seems more like well-meaning torture than treatment. The cauterization of his temples with white hot irons, performed later that year away from Assisi, and a subsequent treatment that consisted of piercing his ears to relieve his eye problems are examples of the state of "medical" care in this period.

However ill he may have been, his pains did not touch his soul. It was near San Damiano in the late spring that he composed his "Canticle of Brother Sun." One finds it hard to fathom how he could have written such beautifully radiant poetry while he was so sick and living in such appalling squalor. But compose he did. It was also in this period (June of 1225?) that he interposed himself in a quarrel between Bishop Guido and the mayor of the town of Assisi. He was close to both of them: Guido had been a staunch supporter of Francis from the time the saint divested himself of his worldly goods twenty years earlier. The mayor had a daughter who was a member of Saint Clare's community at San Damiano. When Francis reconciled these two old friends and ended their feud (which might well have been a bloody vendetta in the city) Francis then added his coda about peace to the Canticle. One sees in his line "Blessed are those who endure in peace/for by You they shall be crowned" both a word of praise for his two old friends and an expression of his hope that reconciliation and not enmity will be maintained between the religious and secular powers of his town.

From late summer of 1225 to early June in 1226 Francis traveled to various places in central Italy either in obedience to ecclesiastical summons or to seek help for his health. By late August or early September of 1226 it was clear that his health was ebbing and that death was not far away. He returned to Assisi and was housed first in the palace of bishop Guido who was away at the time on pilgrimage. In September, sure that he would soon die, Francis insisted that he be taken from Guido's residence so that he could die among his brothers at the Portiuncula. His final wish was granted and to that place where his movement had begun he moved with less than a month to live. It is in that final period of his life that he appended the new verses to his "Canticle of Brother Sun":

Be praised, My Lord, for our sister, bodily death
    Whom no one living can escape.
Woe to those who die in sin!
Blessed are those who discover thy holy will
    The second death will do them no harm.

It is worthwhile thinking about those lines for a moment. While Francis embraces death as a "sister" he in no way sentimentalizes death. He sees death as an inevitable finale to life; the fate of every person. His mind, however, immediately turns to something worse than death: dying outside the grace of God. Such a state leads to the second death, which is damnation. One must read those salutary lines against the background of his public life as a man of penitential preaching — a life he undertook when he "left the world." There was no doubt in the mind or heart of Francis that the end of the earthly pilgrimage was to seek the embrace of God. While Francis embraced the Christ of the cross he knew by instinct that the meaning of the cross was salvation: "By thy holy cross you have redeemed the world" was a sentiment on his lips. Death, for

Francis, had an eschatological meaning: it was a transit either to God or away from God. What Saint Francis says in these few verses is a condensed version of what, in the two recensions of his letters to the men and women of penance, he says so urgently: we must die reconciled to God and the church so that the Evil One may not "snatch us away" for all eternity.

In that final month of his life there is a charming moment in which the human side of Francis shines forth clearly. He had a deep friendship with an aristocratic Roman woman, Jacoba of Settesoli, who came to him when he was lingering near death. At his request, she brought some things to prepare his body after death as well as some pastries that he enjoyed. She arrived in time to find him alive (one account says that Francis dispensed with the rule about no women being allowed in the cloister by calling her "Brother" Jacoba) and stayed with him until his death. According to the Franciscan historians Lady Jacoba stayed on in Assisi until her death some years later (1239? 1273?). She was buried in the lower church of the basilica of Saint Francis in Assisi. In 1933 her remains were re-interred in an urn, and the urn was placed in the crypt adjacent to the tomb of the saint himself.

When Francis himself was clear in his own mind that his death was imminent, he made his farewell to Saint Clare and her sisters at San Damiano and prepared for death at the Portiuncula. Francis asked that the friars strip off his clothes and place him on the bare earth after his death. He was to rest there, Bonaventure says in the *Legenda Major,* for the space of time it takes to "walk a leisurely mile." We cannot overstate how profoundly that final act of nudity brings certain themes of his life to a fitting conclusion. The idea of nudity is deep in the consciousness of all of the great Christian mystics. Saint John of the Cross, many centuries later, would say in his "Sayings of Light and Love" that we should follow Jesus Christ "in becoming like Him, imitating his life, actions, and virtues, and the form of his nakedness and purity of spirit."

Francis, lying on the ground in his nakedness, recapitulated his own birth when he came into this world, like Jesus and every child naked to the world. When Francis wished to begin his new life, turning away from the world, he stripped himself naked before his own father, Pietro, and the Bishop of Assisi, Guido, as part of his second birth as a wanderer for Christ. Once, he walked through a town naked with a halter around his neck to show his humility. All of his commentators, as we have seen, linked his nakedness to two ancient themes: the nakedness of Adam before the Fall (emphasizing the innocence of Francis) and the ancient theme of "following the naked Christ nakedly" — a sentiment as old as Saint Jerome.

To these themes we now have Francis, giving away everything including his poor clothes, to be embraced by Mother Earth whom he had hymned so beautifully in his preaching and in his poetry. His nakedness is also a gestural reminder that it is from the clay of the earth we come and it is to the earth we return: "Ashes to ashes; dust to dust." Hidden in that gesture, to be sure, was a rebuke to the Cathars and the others who deprecated the materiality of God's creation. We, like Jesus, are born of the earth into the material world from which shines the beauty of creation.

On his last evening on this world, Francis, surrounded by his faithful friars and "Brother" Jacoba asked for someone to bring a Mass book to him and read from the Gospel of Saint

John appointed for Holy Thursday: "Before the feast of Passover, Jesus realized that his hour had come for him to pass from this world to the Father. He had loved his own in this world and would show his love for them to the end" (Jn 13:1). Saint Bonaventure, in his *Legenda Major*, says that Francis responded by reciting Psalm 141 (142) from the beginning until the end; the last verse of that psalm reads, "Lead me out of my prison, that I may give thanks to your name./Then the just shall gather around me/because you have been good to me" (142:8).

All the ancient sources say that skylarks flew onto the roof of his cell and sang for him as he died. Brother Elias's letter about the death of Francis says that he died during the first hour of the night (after sunset) on October 3, 1226. Since the new day was reckoned as beginning after sunset his death has been memorialized on October 4, which is when his feast is celebrated unto this day. Elias went on to say that he was buried the next day. He was first buried in the church of San Giorgio, the church where, as a child, he was instructed by the parish priests in whatever formal learning he acquired.

Less than two years later, Pope Gregory IX would come in person to Assisi for the formal canonization of Francis. The solemn ceremonies were carried out on July 16. The solemn Bull of Canonization (*Mira Circa Nos*) was issued from the city of Perugia on August 14, 1228, stipulating October 4 as the feast day of the saint. The process of canonization seems to have happened in a most speedy fashion, but it must be remembered that the pope, who had assumed his office in 1227, had a close relationship to the saint. Gregory's two predecessors, Honorius III (died 1227) and Innocent III (died 1216), had both given their approval to the Franciscan way of life. Innocent did so after meeting Francis and seeing the now lost primitive rule, and Honorius approved the rule of 1223.

The future pope was born into a noble family in Segni in 1170. Count, later Cardinal, Ugolino (Hugolin) was a blood relative of both Popes Innocent III and Alexander IV. He was made cardinal-bishop of Ostia in 1206 and as such became dean of the college of cardinals. He served the papacy as a legate but, more importantly for the story of Saint Francis, he took a keen interest in the rising importance of the new religious orders that were so much a feature of church reform. Above all, the pope had a close relationship to the early Franciscan *religio*. He was the first cardinal protector of the Franciscan Order. He provided a helping hand in the shaping of the so-called 1223 "sealed rule" *(Regula Bullata)* of the Franciscans. He aided in the adaptation of this rule for the Third Order and was responsible for the rule (1218/1219) for the Poor Clares.

Saint Bonaventure tells us that it was under the pope's initiative that the testimony of miracles performed through the intercession of the saint was gathered and presented to the cardinals who "seemed less favorable to his [that is, Francis's] cause" so that with "the unanimous advice and assent of his confreres and of all the prelates who were then in the curia, he decreed that Francis should be canonized." Whether Bonaventure notes that unanimity as part of his own struggle with those who were not favorably disposed to the Mendicants (as those at the University of Paris who did not like the Mendicants possessing academic chairs surely were) or not is a moot point. What we do know is that six years later, in 1234, Pope Gregory IX did stipulate that all canonizations were under the sole power and process of the papacy — a decree that went back as early as the papacy of Alexander III at the end of the twelfth century but became normative only in Gregory's day.

One more step in the posthumous honor of the saint occurred in 1230. The friars assembled in Assisi for their general chapter. On May 25 they transferred the saint's body from its resting place at the church of San Giorgio to rebury it in the lower church of the massive basilica being erected in the city of Assisi. Brother Elias of Cortona had started the project in 1228, the year of the canonization, but the church (or, more properly, the churches, since there is both a lower and upper church) was not finished until 1253. Francis is buried in the lower church decorated with some early frescoes including a famous enthroned Madonna with Saint Francis done by Cimabue. Later fourteenth-century frescoes come from the workshop of Giotto and the hand of Pietro Lorenzetti. The fourteenth-century depiction of Saint Martin of Tours was done by Simone Martini. Near the tomb of Francis are buried his four earliest companions, Brothers Leo, Masseo, Rufino, and Angelo. The remains of Lady Jacoba of Settesoli, as we already noted, are enshrined nearby.

It is worthwhile to note in passing that before the actual canonization in 1228 Pope Gregory IX issued another official letter. This was a papal bull asking the Catholic faithful to donate alms in order to construct a church in honor of Saint Francis to be built on donated land in Assisi. A year after the canonization he issued another bull taking the ownership and protection of the basilica under his own person. In a stroke he relieved the friars from "owning" the building. The fact that Gregory started a campaign for alms before the actual canonization harkens back to the ancient custom of enshrining the remains of a saint in a special shrine church while also signaling that he had every intention of canonizing Francis.

The upper church (badly damaged in the recent earthquake of 1997) contains a famous cycle of frescoes depicting the life and miracles of Saint Francis. That cycle, once attributed to Giotto, is now attributed to an anonymous "Master of the Saint Francis Cycle." It is quite likely that the work was done under the patronage of Pope Nicholas IV (died 1292) who himself was a Franciscan.

That Francis's body should have ended up in such a massive edifice has long irritated some who love the Poor Little Man of Assisi, since the church itself seems surrounded by a redoubtable complex of buildings that cluster around it: a huge convent ("Sacro Convento") and old papal residence (1300); a cloister built in 1476; and an ugly eighteenth-century refectory. Be that as it may, the pilgrims still come to look at the church with its art and pray at the massive but plain tomb of the saint, which was restored in 1925.

The Franciscan charisma turned into monument did not stop with the building of the basilica of Saint Francis. The basilica of Saint Clare, built to house her body in 1257, stands above the foundations of the old church of San Giorgio which was Francis's parish church. Within that church is the oratory of the crucifix that contains the great painted crucifix that "spoke" to Francis; it once hung in the church of San Damiano. Above the city on the flanks of Monte Subasio is the hermitage of the Carceri (literally: the "prison cells"), enlarged by the redoubtable fifteenth-century Observant Franciscan preacher, Saint Bernardine of Siena, where Saint Francis retired for contemplative meditation. The hermitage is now a small friary and one of the most beautiful spots in the area. Below the town is the beautiful church and convent of San Damiano where Saint Clare once lived. Near that spot is the place purported to be where Saint Francis composed the larger part of his "Canticle of Brother Sun." Below the town in the valley is the ugliest church in the entire environs: the massive baroque basilica of Saint Mary of the Angels, finished in the seventeenth century and rebuilt in the nineteenth century, which houses a rare treasure: a tiny romanesque chapel that stood in the days of Saint Francis — the "Little Portion" where he would gather his brethren. It was in that tiny chapel that the great mystic Simone Weil first felt compelled to kneel down and pray.

One of the things that makes Assisi such an attractive place is that the old city has managed to retain much of its medieval character. The civic buildings around the main square are still there; the cathedral of San Rufino may still be visited as can the Benedictine house, which reminds visitors of the monastic presence that existed long before the lifetime of the saint and whose generosity helped him in his earliest days.

Apart from the clogs of day trippers, Assisi is enhanced by the serious pilgrims who come not only for the natural beauty of the area (and beautiful it is) but for the places made sacred by the presence of the saint. It is a place of both ecumenical and interreligious pilgrimage. Once while staying in Assisi a pilgrim, a Swiss Protestant, said to me that Francis was her saint also. She was, of course, right. It was fitting that Pope John Paul II, in 1986, called for a meeting of the world's religious leaders to come to Assisi to pray for peace, as John Paul II did again in 2001. It was Assisi, after all, where Francis first tried to bring peace to a torn world. At those papal meetings Christians, Jews, Muslims, Buddhists, Hindus, as well as peoples representing other religious traditions met and prayed. Somehow the image of Francis and the caliph meeting together in peace hovers over such gatherings.

CHAPTER EIGHT

Francis Reconsidered

Saints should be judged guilty until proven innocent.

George Orwell

THAT FRANCIS IS ONE of the most loveable of the saints in the entire historical panoply of Christian holiness tempts very little in the way of argument. Within his own lifetime he exhibited a powerful charismatic influence on people best exemplified by the numbers who flocked to join him and his poor brothers, to say nothing of the social classes who felt that attraction. What had started out as an experiment in gospel living became before his death a large movement numbering, within the first order itself, in the thousands.

The literature about the saint began within a few years of his death and continued for some generations. The massive compilation of the stories of Francis extant in Latin from the thirteenth and fourteenth centuries fills a huge book of nearly 800 pages in the *Analecta Franciscana* (volume 10) compiled by Franciscan scholars in the first half of the twentieth century. As those who are most familiar with that literature well know, many of the early legends were written not as charmingly simple examples of hagiography but as works that had a definite point of view about who Francis was and what his intentions were. There is a whole school of studies, not unlike that of New Testament scholarship which seeks to recapture the "historical Jesus," that has debated the meaning of Francis for well over a century.

This extended debate has its origins in a book published by the French Protestant scholar, Paul Sabatier, in the late nineteenth century. His *Life of Saint Francis of Assisi* (English translation, 1894) depicted Francis as a kind of proto-evangelical whose simple life of gospel living was betrayed by the institutional church, which forced his simple vision into the procrustean bed of canonical legislation and papal supervision. To paraphrase Renan: Francis preached the gospel and we ended up with the Franciscan Order. Rome paid Sabatier a backhanded compliment for the audacity of his claim: they put his work on the index of forbidden books.

Nobody today defends Sabatier's thesis in its entirety. Like many classic theories about the nature of history or a moment in history (think of Jacob Burckhardt on the Renaissance) it is a sounding board against which thinkers play. As a consequence, a good deal of Franciscan historiography is done with Sabatier's ghost as an offstage presence. To what degree were Francis and his ideals betrayed by the institutionalization of his insights? How explain the anguished cry of Francis at the end of his *Testament* about not putting glosses on his rule or saying that there was another one? Was the admission of scholars to his *religio* a slippery slope toward a class structure? What happened to the ideal of absolute poverty? In the generations after Francis, did not the fight about the character of poverty always look back to the figure of Francis himself for justification? Was the clericalization of the Order consonant with Francis's aims even if he himself held the priesthood in the highest esteem? Is the whole subsequent history of the Franciscan Order(s) merely a proof of the Weberian thesis about the routinization of charisma?

Those questions are still discussed, but the recent trend toward a close reading of Francis's own writings and away from a too single-minded gaze on the early writings about him has helped to frame issues more crisply. As these pages have earlier argued, any close examination of his writings, *pace* Sabatier, show unambiguously that Francis was an orthodox Catholic believer who clearly and persistently incorporated the reforming spirit of Lateran Council IV into his teaching. Francis had nothing in common with those movements of his day that veered toward heterodox claims of autonomy from either episcopal or papal control. In fact, one could make the case that his very success — apart from the persuasive power of his own charismatic personality — derived from the confidence that both bishops and popes (as well as future popes) had in him and what he was trying to do. In order to survive, in short, the Franciscan *religio* had to make its peace with the regnant realities of medieval Catholicism.

One of the ironies of the story of Francis is that a good many problems derived from the simple fact that he was a charismatic and compellingly holy figure. After all — and here I merely gloss some titles taken from Bonaventure's major legend of the saint — a "leader" and a "herald" and a "practitioner" of gospel perfection, a "hierarchic man," the angel of the sixth seal, the "perfect follower of Christ" who bore the "seal of the likeness of the crucified Christ" upon his body was someone to be reckoned with. One could multiply such sentiments from earlier sources, culminating in the extravagant book by Bartholomew of Pisa who complied a tedious list of conformities between the life of Francis and the life of Christ; a book, by the way, that would later irritate Martin Luther intensely.

The net result of this focus on Francis is that the meaning of his order was intimately tied to his own meaning. By contrast, the other mendicant orders of the time — the Dominicans, the Carmelites, and the Augustinians to name the major ones — did not focus with such exactitude on their founders but on the particular charisms of the order itself. Thus, for example, while the Dominicans certainly and zealously honored their founder, Dominic Guzman (1170?-1221; canonized 1234), the preaching friars kept their main focus on study and preaching and not on the person of Dominic himself. For their rule of life they adopted the Rule of Saint Augustine.

The Order of Friars Hermits of Saint Augustine were formally organized in the mid-thirteenth century from various small communities that had adopted Augustine's rule — a rule that had already been in use among the regular canons and other monastic movements instituted in the wake of the Gregorian reform. Even though the medieval Augustinians tried to link their order historically to the great bishop of Hippo, in fact they did so only because they wanted to have the authority of Augustine as their founder. The Carmelites, likewise, had a long and complicated history. Their origins can be traced back to hermits living on Mount Carmel in the Holy Land who, when they migrated to Europe, underwent a series of permutations before taking up the mendicant life. It was only with difficulty that they could point to a single founder, so their history was less concerned with a charismatic person. Despite this, like the Augustinians, the Carmelites needed some figure of authority, so they loved to invoke the figure of Elijah the Prophet who had lived on Mount Carmel before the Christian dispensation.

The Franciscans, by contrast, were centrally concerned with the person and the ideals of a single person, Francis of Assisi. The main lines of his vision were clear enough. Francis wanted his followers to live in poverty after the example of the Poor Christ. He wanted them to preach the gospel and he wanted them to be makers of peace and missionaries of goodness. Clearly, he wanted them to remain within, and be exemplars of, Catholic Christianity. He saw them (as did the popes who encouraged them) as Catholic reformers who would carry out the ideals stipulated by the reforming councils held at the Lateran. Their devotional focus would be intensely christological and their missionary strategy would be to preach the gospel everywhere and to all who had not heard of Christ. To shape the movement into a coherent community Francis gave them a Rule.

That the early Franciscans upheld that ideal is beyond question. They filled the cities of Christendom with churches designed to attract people who could hear the gospel. They expanded their efforts not only in Europe but outside the traditional confines of Christian influence. The missionary movement of the period had a deep Franciscan influence. As we have seen, Franciscans were already active in areas of Islamic influence during the lifetime of the saint and the history of the Holy Land, from the time of Francis down to the present day, has been marked by a persistent Franciscan presence. In time the mendicant followers of Francis would make their way east even into China.

Nonetheless, the power of Francis's own life was such that it would fuel various ways of understanding fidelity to the saint. Foremost was the issue of Francis's attitude toward learning and scholarship. Francis had welcomed the Portuguese canon, Anthony of Padua, into his order but warned that his studies should not be undertaken at the expense of "holy poverty." Francis feared that study inevitably demanded the owning of books, life among an educated elite, and all of the infrastructure that study demanded.

Whatever fears Francis may have had, the Franciscan movement attracted brilliant men to the order who have become familiar names among those who study theology. In the century following the death of Francis we need only recall the names Alexander of Hales, Bonaventure, Peter John Olivi, John Duns Scotus, and William of Ockham. Some of these figures were professors at the University of Paris, which was the center of academic learning in the thirteenth century. That they became professors was, of course, a paradox, since holding chairs at prestigious centers like Paris was exactly what Francis did not have in mind for his companions.

Not all the followers of Francis were pleased or edified by the luminaries of academic learning who called themselves Franciscans. The most vehement protest against academic learning as a corrosive influence on Franciscan poverty came from the pen of the poet Jacopone of Todi (died 1306), who became a Franciscan after the death of his wife sometime in the

1270s. Jacopone belonged to the radical wing of the Franciscans who espoused a severe dedication to poverty and self-denial. In one of his "lauds" he wrote a tercet that summed up a certain disdain for learning:

> That's the way it is — not a shred left of the spirit
> of the Rule!
> In sorrow and grief I see Paris destroy Assisi stone
> by stone.
> With all their theology they've led the Order down
> a crooked path.

Friars like Jacopone emphasized withdrawal from the world, simple poverty, identification with the poor, and so on. Some of them were drawn into the contemplative withdrawal of hermit life. Some of their numbers caused fissures in the Franciscan Order itself so that by the fourteenth century there were small conventicles who were not only in rebellion against authorities within the Order but against episcopal and papal authority. The story of those Spiritual Franciscans is a complicated one and beyond the scope of this study. Suffice it to say that despite the suppression of some of these groups (a few even went to the stake in the fourteenth century) that radical strain of otherworldliness, rejection of wealth, and literal if eccentric views of gospel living would never die out; it would reappear in other forms in the sixteenth century in strains of the Radical Reformation after Luther.

The various branches of the Franciscan Order, both male and female, would persist down to the present day. The various orders of friars, contemplative nuns (the Poor Clares), sisters, and laypersons who follow the Third Order rules of the Franciscan family still enrich the life of the church. But the spirit and teachings of Francis do not reside solely within the confines of the Franciscan Orders. One could argue that radical lay groups like the Catholic Workers reflect to a large degree the simple ideal of the Franciscan *religio.*

We could think of Francis as a kind of spiritual classic in the sense that he should be understood in his own terms as a historical person who lived in a precise historical period but whose meaning is available for other generations to learn about as a source of Christian wisdom. That Francis was a medieval person is beyond dispute. Not to understand him against everything that was going on in his age — the rise of urban life, the birth of the universities, the crusades, the reforming councils, the culture of mercantilism — is not to understand him at all. But to assert his social location is not the same thing as saying that he represents only a medieval type.

What, broadly speaking, does Francis teach the generations that followed beyond him?

First, when we view Francis in the context of his own life we see a person who sought to live the gospel life by a series of experiments which he undertook by drawing on the models available to him. We see in his life a kind of evolution in his own spiritual journey in which he makes use of the ways of Christian living available to him. For a period in his life he lived as a man of penance by withdrawing from the world, serving the poor, the sick, and the lepers while spending his time in prayer and retreat. For a period he even took up the life of the traditional hermit, complete with the traditional garb of the hermit: the staff, the leather shoes, the rough tunic, and the belt. After hearing the gospel challenge of living completely poorly he decided that was the life for him, but even then he fashioned himself in a model that was available to him: he fancied himself a knight errant, not bearing arms but bearing the cross and serving his ideal woman, Lady Poverty. In other words, Francis replicated in his own life aspects of Christian reform that were abroad in the culture.

In that sense, Francis drew upon the hagiographical memory of the Christian tradition to find a way of life that was compatible with the intuitions that he had received as a person who wished to follow the gospel. Neither his life nor his strategies, in short, were born without reference to the currents abroad in the times in which he lived. It is true that he did not find his place in the traditional options open to him. He did not enter monastic life; he did not seek out ordination and join the canons regular; he did not satisfy himself with one of the traditional "rules of life" that were already approved by the church. In fact, insisting upon and actually obtaining a new rule was a rather singular fact about his life. Nonetheless he did draw on the tradition in his search for a life appropriate for him.

To understand Francis, then, one must understand him against the background from which he came and against the sources available to him. The great lesson is that while Francis did do something new, his newness cannot be detached from the tradition that made his originality possible. Further, his newness was also an attempt not to replicate the mistakes others had made. He fought hard to keep his life and that of his followers within the Catholic tradition — to live, as he said, *more catholico,* "after the Catholic manner." He did not want to end up as one of those marginal heretical groups who so reacted against the abuses within the church that they found themselves totally alienated from the great church itself, as did, for example, the Poor Men of Lyons or the Patarines of Milan.

What was the major insight of Francis that made him an original? Basically, the answer is his understanding of evangelical poverty. Francis did not understand religious poverty as the "sharing of goods" as did the monastic tradition. What Francis wanted to do was to be a person of non-possession: no lands, no income, no saving up "for a rainy day," no possessions beyond what was needed for daily life. This was hardly a new idea in itself but Francis had a deeply realized Christian motive for living in this way. He thought that to live a life of radical poverty was to actually perform the gospel command of Jesus to give up everything for his sake. In that sense, Francis was a biblical literalist.

Furthermore, Francis linked his idea of poverty to his fuller understanding of christology. He saw, among other things, the poverty of Christ's birth, his wandering life in Galilee, and, above all, his passion and death on the cross as the model for his own poverty. He would be as poor as the poor Christ. Beyond that he understood the Incarnation itself as an act of self-giving, as a self-emptying embodied in the simple statement of John that the Word became flesh (Jn 1:14).

While it is true that his emphasis on poverty had a prophetic edge to it in that it was a rebuke to the worldliness of the church and its ministers and as a protest against the commercial rapaciousness of the rising mercantile class (like that of his own father) and the greed of the aristocratic class, his basic motive was christological: he would be poor because Christ was poor.

This insight into the significance of Christ as a person of poverty who is the model to be imitated yields a fuller picture of Francis's own understanding of the gospel. Poverty was the hermeneutical lens through which he read the gospel. It also created the neuralgic point that would create so much tension once his own life led others to him. Discussions about the practice of poverty troubled Francis's fraternity in his own lifetime and in the growth of the order after his death. It is not difficult to see how the tensions arose. For Francis, living a life of poverty was a simple imperative deriving from his conversion — his hearing the gospel. Others may have felt the same call.

The problem arose, however, when one had to face the practical issues that were thrown up on almost a daily basis: what about the need for books for the celebration of the liturgy? How to care for a friar who was sick? How to feed and house friars when they began to increase in numbers? What about the support of learned men who could contribute to the preaching mission of the church — were they to be denied books? One is reminded of a quip made by a follower of Mohandas Gandhi who was another man zealous to live poorly: "If the old man only knew how expensive it is to keep him in his life of poverty!"

The practice of evangelical poverty can be understood under the rubric of traditional asceticism that has had a long and honorable history in the Christian spiritual tradition. Francis did add another note to the practice: that living poorly was a *joy.* One element that can be detected in the early stories of Francis is that his life was characterized by a certain joy. While one can exaggerate this idea (and it has been overblown by some more romantically inclined admirers of the saint), there is in the early legends a joy that Francis expresses in his love for music, his eye for beauty, his reaction to the wonders of creation, his tenderness to dumb animals, his concern for the poor, the sentiments he expresses in his prayers, in his lauds, and, above all, in his famous canticle. It is almost as if by dispossessing himself of his worldly goods he took on a new eye for the beauties of the world and those who inhabit it. Speaking to his own brothers in one of his admonitions (#20) Francis said "Blessed is that religious who takes no pleasure and joy except in the most holy words and deeds of the Lord and with these leads people to the love of God in joy and gladness."

Francis himself, if a story remembered by one of his early friars is correct, underscored the concept of joy in the form of a story. Francis said that perfect joy would not come from hearing that all of the professors of Paris had become friars along with all the prelates and the kings of England. Perfect joy would not come if news arrived that all unbelievers came to the true faith. Perfect joy comes when, rebuffed and left in the darkness of the night, when one seeks shelter, some food, and a place to sleep and is called a stupid beggar to boot, if one might still have "patience and did not become upset, there would be perfect joy in this and true virtue and the salvation of the soul." One has to read that simple story against the picture of Christ who demands that one turn the other cheek as he did when struck and rebuffed while in the hands of Pilate and his soldiers. Behind that story is a whole complex intuition about detachment, forgiveness, humility, and the other virtues that make up the deepest following of Christ.

One cannot understand Francis's following of the poor way

of Christ as an exercise designed only for his own salvation or his own search for spiritual perfection. Francis saw his life as a gift to others. Francis marked his own conversion from the time he resisted his own natural repugnance and turned toward the lepers whom he had until then avoided. In his search to imitate Christ he identified himself with the *minores* — those who were on the bottom of the economic and social scale. In the Rule of 1221 Francis urged his brethren to beg alms because the right to alms was a legacy for the poor guaranteed by Jesus. At the same time, later in that same Rule, he told his friars that when things were asked of them they were to be given without thought of repayment. This was just a variation on his desire to minister to the poor.

It does not take much reflection to see how Francis was a living example of what would become, in modern theological parlance, the "preferential option for the poor." Indeed, it is no exaggeration to say that his whole life was shaped by a conscious decision to be on the side of the poor after the example of the poor Christ. Although it would be a bit tendentious to retroject his life and his identification with the poor into some kind of early liberation theology, it is possible to see his life from the perspective of liberationist thinking in this sense: Francis had a radical vision of the equality of all persons who, after all, were icons of Christ and, as such, had an inherent dignity which demanded that they be treated with justice and out of a sense of love. There is in any radical adoption of this deep christological truth a certain way in which class and social distinctions are deconstructed and relativized. Francis was not one, despite his scrupulous observance of the social norms of the day, who saw more merit in a pope than in a peasant.

One particular form of human solidarity in which Francis took a keen interest was the nurturance of peace among those who were divided by contention. He did that, as we have already seen, by reconciling people in his own hometown, by preaching peace in the towns and villages he visited, and when he even crossed hostile battle lines to speak to the caliph who warred against his fellow Christians. It should not surprise us that his habitual greeting was "Peace" or that the word "peace" and "peacemaker" occurs with some frequency in his writings.

Perhaps the most important reason that Saint Francis caught the imagination of future generations so vividly had more to do with his persona than with anything he wrote or said. The vast majority of people have no imaginary picture of a Saint Augustine (was he befittingly dark skinned?) or an Anselm of Canterbury or Bernard of Clairvaux in their head. Others may have a completely imaginary picture of a Saint Antony of the desert due to the vivid artistic representations in the tradition or they know that Saint Jerome translated the Bible into Latin and had a sharp tongue. But in the case of Francis we think we know what he looked like, how he dressed, what his interests were, and the most popular stories about him. To put it simply: we can imagine Saint Francis even if that image has been shaped in part by the huge artistic reservoir we have at our disposal.

There was keen interest in the person and gestures of Francis both in his lifetime and within a few years of his death. When Elias of Cortona began immediately to erect a fitting basilica to honor the saint and his tomb he had the shrewd good sense to know that this was not just one more saint — this was a person who would attract crowds of pilgrims and visitors in vast numbers.

Thomas of Celano sketched out a portrait of the saint in his first life of the saint in a highly stylized fashion (borrowing from a hagiographical portrait of Bernard of Clairvaux), describing him as short, thin, with fine teeth and a small beard on an elongated face — a portrait that may have inspired the one drawn by Berlingheri for the Pescia altarpiece which was done in 1235, only a decade after the saint's death. That altarpiece, and the famous fresco of the saint in the *Sacro Specchio* at the Benedictine monastery of Subiaco (early thirteenth century?), mark the beginning of a huge artistic tradition that would run from that time down through the baroque into the rococo period. The various representations of the saint, especially Saint Francis receiving the stigmata, are set pieces in the history of art. They are also, of course, highly idealized and imaginatively constructed attempts to grasp the meaning of the saint.

There is another way of thinking about the persona of Francis. One could say that his life (and, to a real extent, his body) was a kind of exegesis of the scriptures and an attempt to live out the imitation of Christ. While it is true that Francis is depicted in the sources as an intuitive explicator of the scriptures and while it is equally true that his writings are saturated with excerpts from the Bible, it is even more true — and more important — to understand that Francis was more a performer of the Word of God than a commentator upon it. In a certain sense, Francis was a scriptural literalist in that he saw the gospels as giving him precise instructions about how to live his life. It would not be too audacious to say that the stigmata were a kind of writing on the body of Francis — a kind of reversal or mirror image of the passion story.

If the gospel says that a follower of Jesus should go abroad preaching and teaching without goods or that he should leave everything and follow Christ, Francis saw those dicta as precise instructions about how to live one's life. The gospel, for Francis, was not a book for meditation but marching orders for living. Such an approach to the call of the gospel is certainly not peculiar to Francis, but what was singular about his reaction to the gospel, as Bernard McGinn and others have pointed out, was his ability to combine into a single whole the demands for repentance, preaching, and service to the poor with the absolute centrality of the cross. In that sense, Francis's understanding of the emptying of the Word in the incarnation, the solidarity of all men and women because of the incarnation, and the self-emptying on the cross are all part of the same seamless fabric.

Francis understood that preaching meant communication. He also understood that the way one lives, the fashion in which a person interacts with others, the picture one presents to the world — these are all forms of communication. He put this theory of communication succinctly in instructions he once gave to some of his brothers as they were about to enter a town: "Preach and, if necessary, use words."

The striking singularity of Francis did get lost over the centuries when Francis himself faded into the background while the friars and their struggles to define themselves came to the fore. By the dawn of the sixteenth century it was the friars who felt the lash of the pen of Erasmus. In the Reformation the mendicants were swept away in those countries most affected by the reformers. The Enlightenment had scorn for Francis and his followers (see the indifference of Goethe or the vitriol of Voltaire), only to see them rediscovered in the age of the Romantics. Alas, many of the portraits of Francis in the nineteenth and twentieth centuries projected onto Francis all of the artists' love for Umbrian countrysides, Italian sunshine, and quaint animals.

Others, however, caught a glimpse of Francis the radical. Gandhi understood the persuasive power of his poverty, his love for peace, and his identification with the poor. Simone Weil grasped his self-abandonment and the lure of the cross. She said that entering the little chapel of the Portiuncula forced her, for the first time in her life, to go to her knees in prayer. Dorothy Day and Peter Maurin, founders of that most Franciscan of movements, the Catholic Workers, captured his spirit of generous attention to the poor in whom he saw Christ and his life of disciplined prayer.

Buoyed by the success of the earlier interreligious meeting, Pope John Paul II called for a second meeting to be held in Assisi under the rubric of an "Interreligious Day of Prayer for Peace in the World" on January 24, 2002. The papal invitation went to two hundred leaders of twenty-four different religions. In his opening address to these religious leaders John Paul said that the meeting at Assisi was significant because everything in Assisi "speaks of a singular prophet of peace known as Francis. He is loved not only by Christians but by many other believers and by people, far removed from religion, who identify with his ideals of justice, reconciliation, and peace."

At the conclusion of the day of prayer the representatives gave each other the kiss of peace while the "Canticle of the Creatures" of Saint Francis was sung. A document entitled "The Assisi Decalogue for Peace," composed for the occasion, was sent to all leaders and heads of governments on March 4 of the same year.

The charismatic power of Saint Francis draws quite different people for quite different reasons. The devoutly religious composer Olivier Messiaen (1908-1992) premiered his opera *Saint Francois d'Assise* in Paris in 1983. Divided into eight tableaux, the libretto is not a retelling of the saint's life but rather a series of way stations on the road to God. The justly famous sixth tableau is Francis's "Sermon to the Birds" (Messiaen was a keen bird-watcher and ornithologist) in which Francis "hears" the presence of God in creation. It stands as a contrast to the final two scenes where, against the background of a powerful chorus, Francis receives the stigmata and finally, in the final death scene, he is stretched out like his crucified Lord and is sent upward by the chorus bathed in the light of God.

The publication of Michael Hardt and Antonio Negri's *Empire* (Harvard University Press, 2000) is light miles away in spirit from Messiaen's opera. Negri, an unrepentant communist militant, issued the book as a manifesto for the possibilities of communism on the cusp of the new millennium, a sort of counterpoint to Marx's *Communist Manifesto* of 1848. Negri is convinced that the moment for a communist revolution may be more possible now given the looming oppression of superpowers and the hegemony of multinational corporations. His book has received little attention outside of the hothouse atmosphere of left-wing intellectuals.

What is startling, however, is the epilogue of the book. The militants of the future must work within the vast somewhat amorphous world which, de facto, is. The task of the militant is to shape affective networks within the set of social structures with no illusion of the possibility of transcending them. Who might model such a form of life? In a startling final paragraph

Negri says: consider the work of Francis of Assisi. Francis who opposed "nascent capitalism" not by world-denying forms of asceticism but by a "joyous life, including all of being and nature, the animals, sister moon, brother sun, the birds of the field, the poor and exploited humans, together against the will of power and corruption." This is the kind of revolution Negri wishes to model and hence his final sentence: "This is the irrepressible lightness and joy of being communist."

European romanticism has come full circle in little more than a century. The nineteenth-century *bien pensants* wanted a Francis who communed with nature untrammeled by the constrictive power of the church and its dogma. They were quite willing, as Paul Sabatier said in the preface of his 1893 biography of the saint, to leave the shrine, the relics, and the cult of the saint to the Catholic Church; they saw a Francis who was evangelical, a lover and composer of poetry, and the incarnation of the best of Mediterranean sun-loving culture. A generation later, that most cynical of Mediterraneans, Benito Mussolini, would call Francis the "most Italian of saints; the most saintly of the Italians." At the end of the century, the same romantic figure of Francis shows up as a joyful militant who is a paradigm for those who lead the vanguard of activists toward a communist utopia.

What the romantic and communist visions of Francis have in common is a Francis outside the world in which he lived and apart from the sources that nourished his life and his vision. He was neither a lover of nature nor a utopian (although some of his followers, the Spiritual Franciscans, may well have been). He was simply a little Umbrian touched by the mysterious power of grace who had a revolutionary idea: to live the life of the Christ of the gospels as closely and as literally as he could. In that sense, Francis was a radical fundamentalist. Francis performed the gospel so perfectly that he became the saint whom we recognize so well today.

Some years ago Frances Young, the Methodist theologian from Great Britain, wrote a little book called *Virtuoso Theology.* She likened the Christian life to the performance of music. The Word of God is like a musical score. It may be studied and there may be great efforts to establish a clear text and the intention of the text (the work, respectively, of the exegete or theologian and, by parallel, the musicologist) but the full meaning of the text appears only when it is performed. Fidelity to the text is the bottom line, but there is a difference between a beginner plunking away at Mozart's *Eine Kleine Nachtmusik* and the same piece at the hands of a seasoned performer. Some read so deeply into the mind of the composer that we honor such a person as a musical virtuoso. It is safe to say that Francis was such a virtuoso whose music is still heard today and enriches us in the hearing.

CHAPTER NINE

A Reading Essay

THE SHEER VOLUME of research done on Saint Francis and the Franciscan movement is such that no single scholar can easily keep up with it. There are learned journals in a variety of languages and popular magazines under Franciscan auspices in many parts of the world. One valuable resource for keeping up with Franciscan scholarship is *Greyfriars Review,* which provides essays in English translations of the more significant research done in the various languages.

What appears below is only a sampling of literature, all in English, of books which in my estimation are helpful in understanding the life of the saint. Many more particular studies have not been included, and of the books mentioned, some are more reliable than others. Comments made about the books will attempt, in obedience to Francis's love for *cortesia,* gently to indicate which of the books are the better ones. In my years of reading about Francis the tradition of Italian scholarship have been most illuminating for me. Those books and essays are not mentioned in this rather brief survey but scholars in matters Franciscan will recognize my debt to those scholars.

The single best and most indispensable resource for serious English-language students for the study of Saint Francis is a four-volume compilation edited by three Franciscan friars (Regis Armstrong, Wayne Hellmann, and William Short) that provides, in fresh new translations, every text by and about Francis of Assisi for the period up to 150 years after the saint's death in 1226. The titles of the volumes are: *Francis of Assisi: The Saint* (1999); *Francis of Assisi: The Founder* (2000); *Francis of Assisi: The Prophet* (2001); and *Francis of Assisi: Index* (2002). All of the volumes are published by New City Press in New York. They contain all of the writings of the saints; legends about him; liturgical texts; papal documents; and testimonies about him from extra-Franciscan sources. Those four volumes replace the old and somewhat inadequate *Saint Francis of Assisi: Omnibus of Sources* (recently reprinted from the one volume 1973 edition in two volumes by Franciscan University Press in 2002) whose main value today is the charts provided to identify where certain stories of Francis either appear or do not appear in the various legenda.

There has been a notable shift recently towards a close examination of Francis's own writings. Regis Armstrong published *Francis and Clare: The Complete Works* (New York: Paulist, 1982), which is a compendium of the writings of both Francis and Clare with useful introductions and notes. The same scholar also published a close study of those writings in *Saint Francis of Assisi: Writings for a Gospel Life* (New York: Crossroad, 1994). In addition, Edith van den Goorbergh and Theodore Zweerman's *Respectfully Yours: Signed and Sealed Francis of Assisi* (St. Bonaventure, N.Y.: Franciscan Institute, 2001) has some excellent close readings of some of Francis's own texts arguing that there is a complexity to them not always recognized at first glance.

Clare of Assisi did not receive the full study she deserves in this present book on Francis but there are some fine biographies of her available in English for those who wish to know more about this extraordinary woman. In 1993 the Franciscan University Press (Quincy, Ill.) published three lives of the saint: Marco Bertoli's *Clare of Assisi;* Margaret Carney's *The First Franciscan Woman: Clare of Assisi and Her Form of Life;* and Ingrid Peterson's *Clare of Assisi: A Biographical Study.* The indefatigable Regis Armstrong has also assembled an excellent resource of historical documents on Clare: *Clare of Assisi: Early Documents* (New York: Paulist, 1988).

The tradition of modern biographies of Saint Francis must begin with Paul Sabatier's study of 1894 translated into English as *Life of Saint Francis of Assisi* (New York: Scribner, 1906). For an excellent study of the romantic presuppositions of Sabatier, see the important study: C. J. Talar. "Saint of Authority and Saint of the Spirit," in *Sanctity and Secularity during the Modernist Period: Six Perspectives on Hagiography circa 1900.* Edited by L. Barmann and C. Talar. Subsidia Hagiographica #79 (Brussels: Société des Bollandistes, 1999), 131-150.

Sabatier's controversial life of the saint provoked a Catholic response by Johannes Jørgensen's 1912 biography in English of the saint, *Saint Francis of Assisi: A Biography* which went through many editions and remained a highly popular work. Gilbert Keith Chesterton's biography, written in the 1930s, is short on fact but, typical of Chesterton, is still highly readable and not infrequently possessed of brilliant insights. As a young man the Greek novelist Nikos Kazantzakis visited the elderly

Danish writer, Jørgensen, in Assisi and, inspired by their conversations, published a fictionalized biography of the saint in 1962 which reflected more of the vitalism of Zorba the Greek than Francis himself.

Omer Englebert's *Saint Francis of Assisi* (Chicago: Franciscan Herald, 1965), translated from the French, was a more rigorous historical study but today seems dated. Helen Moak managed the daunting task of abridging Arnaldo Fortini's five-volume Italian biography of the saint into a single volume: *Francis of Assisi* (New York: Crossroad, 1981). Fortini, the long-time mayor of Assisi, had mined the archives of the city for decades and, through his work, found many important data about the life of Francis.

The novelist and literary figure Julien Green wrote a lyrical biography of the saint entitled *God's Fool: The Life and Times of Saint Francis of Assisi* (New York: Harper & Row, 1985), which is still a joy to read. Adolph Holl's *The Last Christian* (New York: Doubleday, 1980) is an attempt to recast Francis as a radical reforming Christian set against the institution of both church and world. A more convincing case was made by Leonardo Boff's *Saint Francis* (New York: Crossroad, 1984) who was himself a Franciscan friar and a prominent liberation theologian.

More recently there has been a spate of Francis biographies of varying quality. Three excellent works by recognized scholars must be mentioned: Raoul Manselli, *Saint Francis of Assisi* (Chicago: Franciscan Herald, 1988), and Chiara Frugoni, *Francis of Assisi* (New York: Continuum, 1998) represent excellent examples of contemporary Franciscan scholarship in Italy while Michael Robson, *Saint Francis of Assisi: The Legend and the Life* (London: Chapman, 1997), is a superb work by a British friar and scholar. A more modest but stimulating work is Pierre Brunette's *Francis of Assisi and His Conversions* (Quincy, Ill.: Franciscan University Press, 1997), which studies (note the plural in his title) the stages of Francis's journey.

More popular works written recently tend to conflate the later legends into a biographical whole, as does Valerie Martin's *Salvation: Scenes from the Life of St. Francis* (New York: Knopf, 2001) and Adrian House's *Francis of Assisi: A Revolutionary Life* (New York: Hidden Spring/Paulist, 2001). Marginally better is Donald Spoto's *Reluctant Saint: The Life of Francis of Assisi* (New York: Viking, 2002), which does show a familiarity with the critical scholarly literature.

The life of Francis is intimately connected to the growth of the Franciscan Order. The writings about the saint are frequently shaped by differing understandings of the mind of Francis, which has given rise to the knotty "Franciscan Question" debated by scholars for more than a century. A useful guide through the skein of writings after Francis may be found in Jacques Dalarun's *The Misadventure of Francis of Assisi: Towards a Historical Use of the Franciscan Legends* (St. Bonaventure, N.Y.: Franciscan Institute, 2002). There are some classic studies of the origin and growth of the Franciscan *religio:* Cajetan Esser, *The Origins of the Franciscan Order* (Chicago: Franciscan Herald, 1970), Rosalind Brooke, *Early Franciscan Government* (Cambridge: Cambridge University Press, 1959), and John Moorman, *A History of the Franciscan Order* (Oxford: Oxford University Press, 1968). David Burr, *The Spiritual Franciscans: From Protest to Persecution in the Century after Saint Francis* (University Park, Pa.: Pennsylvania State University Press, 2001), is an excellent study of the rise of the radical Franciscans.

Finally, notice should be given to more particularized studies of the saint and his spirituality. Roger Sorrell's *St. Francis of Assisi and Nature* (New York: Oxford University Press, 1988) is an excellent study of the nature stories and their background. Octavian Schmucki, *The Stigmata of St. Francis* (St. Bonaventure, N.Y.: Franciscan Institute, 1991), is a careful historical investigation of the phenomenon of the stigmata. Bernard McGinn has excellent pages on the place of Francis in the history of Christian mysticism (with an excellent bibliography in the notes) in *The Flowering of Mysticism: Men and Women in the New Mysticism — 1200-1350* (New York: Crossroad, 1998), 42-64. William Short's *Poverty and Joy: The Franciscan Tradition* (Maryknoll, N.Y.: Orbis, 1999) is a readable survey of the Franciscan tradition as is the somewhat more ambitious work of Anton Rotzetter, Willibrod-Christian Van Dijk, and Thaddeus Matura, *Gospel Living: Francis of Assisi Yesterday and Today* (St. Bonaventure, N.Y.: Franciscan Institute, 1994).

The Prayer of Saint Francis

Lord:
Make me an instrument of your peace.
Where there is hatred, let me sow love.
Where there is injury, pardon,
Where there is discord, union,
Where there is doubt, faith,
Where there is error, truth,
Where there is despair, hope,
where there is sadness, joy,
Where there is darkness, light.
O Divine Master,
Grant that I may not so much seek to be consoled
*   as to console;*
to be understood, as to understand;
to be loved, as to love;
for it is in giving that we receive,
it is in pardoning that we are pardoned,
And it is in dying that we are born to eternal life. Amen.

THE ABOVE PRAYER, attributed to Saint Francis of Assisi, is one of the best known and most quoted prayers of modern times. Entering the phrase "The Prayer of Saint Francis" into a standard Internet search engine will result in over a thousand sites. Many religious organizations post the prayer on the Web; various musicians have set the prayer to music and recorded it on discs or tapes; it is found, set to music, in many hymnbooks; the prayer and variations of it are part of the spiritual literature of Alcoholics Anonymous; it is found in various sites of spiritual healing, prayer groups, New Age sites, and groups that espouse peacemaking or spiritual forms of therapy.

It comes as a shock to many people to discover that the prayer, however much it reflects the Franciscan sensibility, was written in the early twentieth century. Furthermore, in its first published form it was not even associated with the saint. How that association with Saint Francis arose and how the prayer spread is imperfectly understood even though the main lines are clear.

Evidently the prayer was published as an unsigned contribution to a small popular magazine in Normandy in France in 1913. In 1915 the Marquis de la Rochetulon, the founder of a Catholic weekly called *Souvenir Normand* sent the prayer to Pope Benedict XV along with a few other prayers on the subject of peace. It is not clear if the Marquis had written the prayer himself or found it circulating in his native Normandy. On January 20, 1916, the prayer was published in the Vatican newspaper *Osservatore Romano*. A week later the French Catholic newspaper *La Croix* reprinted the prayer — a common enough practice in the midst of the horrors of World War I.

In those early appearances there was no connection to Saint

Francis of Assisi. In fact, the prayer was directed to the Sacred Heart of Jesus, then a widespread and enormously influential form of devotion to the humanity of Christ (the basilica of Sacre-Coeur in Paris would not be finally finished until 1919). How then did this prayer for peace become associated with Saint Francis?

Shortly after the Roman publication of the prayer in *Osservatore Romano*, a French Franciscan had a poster made up for the benefit of the Third Order of Saint Francis (the lay branch of the Franciscan family) depicting Saint Francis holding the Rule for the Third Order in one hand and the Prayer for Peace in the other. Under the prayer was a note of its source *(Souvenir Normand)* and this annotation: "This prayer sums up Franciscan ideals and also represents a response to the urgent needs of our age." Evidently, from this first connection, the prayer became associated with the name of Francis. Quite possibly (but this is only a surmise) the association became concretized through the network of Third Order fraternities.

Leonardo Boff's recent meditative book on this prayer from which much of the above information is derived (*The Prayer of Saint Francis* [Maryknoll, N.Y.: Orbis, 2001]) argues that the prayer in fact does have a close affinity not only to the spiritual message of Saint Francis but also to its style. Francis loved to articulate disjunctions in his prayers and paraphrases of prayers. Boff points especially to the twenty-seventh *Admonition* of the saint. Using contrasts to show how virtue overcomes vice Francis says: Where there is charity and wisdom/there is neither fear nor ignorance; where there is patience and humility/there is neither anger nor disturbance. Francis includes six such contrasts. One finds the same kind of disjunctions in the saint's "Praise of the Virtues." Of course, this is not to argue that the *Admonitions* are a direct source for the prayer but only to suggest that the style of the prayer, with its contrasts, is concord with the style of the saint.

As of this writing there is still ongoing research into the origins and dispersion of this prayer but for now we will be content to allow this prayer to bear the name of the saint in popular usage — it is a fitting tribute to his generous soul.

Index

Acre, 43, 60, 62

Acts of the Apostles, 26, 45

Adam: nakedness of, 20-21, 98, 113; naming the animals, 97

Agnes of Bohemia, 39

Alexander III, 28, 116

Alexander IV, 83, 115

Alexander of Hales, 125

alms, 13, 22, 28, 42, 56, 116; begged by Franciscans, 35-36, 44, 66, 69, 132; Clare living on, 38-39, 43-44

Analecta Franciscana, 120

Ancona, 60

Angelo, Brother, 116

animals: and Francis, 92-99, 104-5, 131, 137; in hagiographic tradition, 97-98, 105

Anselm of Canterbury, Saint, 77, 133

Anthony of Padua, 59-60, 125

Antony, Saint, 23, 133

Aristotle, 94

Armstrong, Regis, 141

Arnold, Matthew, vii

asceticism, 18-19, 87, 93, 130, 138

Assisi, 1-7, 15, 38-39, 73, 118-19; archives of, 63, 143; Francis in, 22-23, 100, 109-11; "Interreligious Day of Prayer" in (2002), 136; lepers in, 10-13

"Assisi Decalogue for Peace, The," 136

Athanasius, Saint, 23

Augustine, Saint, 6, 32, 133; Rule of, 57, 123

Augustinians, 123-24

Barmann, L., 142

Bartholomew of Pisa, 123

Basil, Saint, 32

basilica of: Saint Francis, 2, 14, 39, 62, 112, 116-17, 133; Saint Mary Major, 76; Saint Mary of the Angels, 118

Beguines, 37, 45

Benedict, Saint, 24, 32, 36

Benedict XV, 147

Benedictines, 23, 31; house of, 118; monastery of, 38, 134

benefice system, 49

Berlingheri altarpiece (Pescia), 93-94, 134

Bernardine of Siena, Saint, 117

Bernard of Clairvaux, 133-34

Bernard of Quintavalle, 30

Bertoli, Marco, 35, 142

Bethlehem, 74-76, 86

birds, and Francis, 74, 93-94, 97, 104-5, 114, 137

Boethius, 7

Boff, Leonardo, 143, 148

Bologna, Francis in, 72

Bonaventure, Saint, 57, 102, 105, 125; *Legenda Major*, 6, 15, 18, 34, 75, 82, 90, 95, 109, 112-15, 122; sermons of, 83; *The Soul's Journey to God*, 86-87, 94-95

Bonhoeffer, Dietrich, 7

Borgo San Sepolcro, 108

British Isles, Lesser Brothers in, 57

Brooke, Rosalind, 144

Brunette, Pierre, 144

Bruno of Cologne, 24

Burckhardt, Jacob, 121

Burckhardt, Walter, 106

Burr, David, 144

Butler, Alban, vii

Cairo, 61

Campostela, shrine of, 37

Canons Regular, 26-27, 45

"Canticle of Brother Sun" (Francis), 99-103, 110-11, 118, 131

"Canticle of the Three Young Men" (Daniel), 103

"Canticles of the Creatures" (Francis), 136

Capuchins, 76

Carceri, hermitage of the, 73, 117

Carmel, Mount, 123-24

Carmelites, 54, 123-24

Carney, Margaret, 37, 142

Catanii, Peter, 65

Cathars, 28, 32, 42, 50, 93, 105, 113

Catherine of Siena, Saint, 87

Catholic Church, 52, 59, 122, 138; Francis's allegiance to, ix, 33-35, 41, 52-55, 67, 69, 122, 124, 128-29; reform of, 26-29, 32, 44, 51, 54, 71, 115, 122-24, 128; on stigmatization, 82-83, 87

Catholic Workers, 127, 136

Chantal, Jeanne Marie De, Saint, 40

Chesterton, Gilbert Keith, 9, 36, 142

China, Franciscans in, 125

Christ, 10-12, 47, 55, 59, 63, 105, 138-39; cross of, 20, 42, 106, 111, 129; in eucharist, 50-51, 53-54, 73; and Francis, 96, 122-23, 131-32, 134-39; humanity of, 76-77, 107, 148; humility of, 42, 53, 74, 77, 131; Incarnation of, 42, 74, 135; as infant, 20, 73-76, 113, 129; nakedness of, 20, 74, 98, 113; passion of, 21, 77, 85-86, 90-91, 129; poverty of, 25, 27, 30, 39, 42, 54, 74, 77, 86, 124, 129-32; teaching of, 12-13, 19-20, 22, 25, 129, 134-35; as Word, 42, 53, 102; wounds of, 79, 82, 85, 87

Christmas, 73-76, 86, 108; and creche tradition, 75-76

Index

Christopher, Saint, 24

church, 44-45, 54; criticism of, 25-26, 121, 129; reform of, 26-27, 32, 48-50, 115

Cimabue, 116

Cioran, Saint, 98

Cistercians, 77

Città di Castello, 109

Civilization of the Renaissance in Italy, The (Burckhardt), 106

Clare (Offreduccio), Saint, 5, 37-40, 43, 46, 100, 102, 109, 112, 117-18, 141-42

Clare of Assisi (Bertoli), 142

Clare of Assisi: A Biographical Study (Peterson), 142

Clare of Assisi: Early Documents (Armstrong), 142

clothing, 19-20, 23; of Clare, 37; of Francis, 25, 126-27; of Franciscan brothers, 36, 45, 69, 90

Colman, Saint, 97

Colossians, Epistle to the, 18

Commedia (Dante), 107

Communist Manifesto (Marx), 137

confession of sins, 42, 50-51, 52, 54

Confessions (Augustine), 6

Conrad of Urslingen, Duke, 4

Consolations of Philosophy (Boethius), 7

creation, and Francis's love for, 92-95, 98-105, 113, 131, 145

cross, 20-22, 42, 86; fourteen stations of, 91; and Francis, 81, 111, 135-36; as symbol, 21, 25, 90

crucifix, Italo-Byzantine, 13, 85

crusaders, 51, 60-61, 63, 90

Crusader States, 43

crusades, 32, 46, 60-61, 127

Cum Secundum, 66

Dalarun, Jacques, 144

Dalmatia, 36

Damien, Peter, 24

Damietta, 60-63

Daniel, Book of, 103

Dante, 21, 46-47, 57, 85, 107

Day, Dorothy, 40, 136

death, Francis on, 100-102, 111-12

De Miseria Humanae Conditionis (Innocent III), 34

Dominicans, 56-57, 107, 123

Dominic Guzman, Saint, 57, 107, 123

Duns Scotus, John, 125

Early Franciscan Government (Brooke), 144

Easter, 51, 77, 90

Eastern church, 48-49

Egypt, Francis in, 63

Elias of Cortona, 57, 65, 79, 81, 84, 109, 114, 116, 133

Elijah the Prophet, 124

Empire (Hardt and Negri), 137

Englebert, Omer, 143

Enlightenment, 135

Ephesians, Epistle to the, 19

Erasmus, 135

Esser, Cajetan, 144

eucharist, 41-42, 50-54, 73, 77

Ezekiel, prophet, 90

Fall (of Adam), 96, 113

fasting, 52, 69, 78, 108

feast of: Assumption of Mary, 77, 108; Exaltation of the Holy Cross, 81, 108; Francis, 83-84, 92, 114. *See also* Christmas, Passover

feudal aristocracy, 2-4, 27

Fioretti, 12, 62, 96

First Franciscan Woman, The: Clare of Assisi and Her Form of Life (Carney), 142

Florence, 15, 57

Flowering of Mysticism, The: Men and Women in the New Mysticism — 1200-1350 (McGinn), 145

Fonte Colombo, 68

Fortini, Arnaldo, 63, 143

France, 4-5, 7, 26, 28, 32, 49, 57

Francis and Clare: The Complete Works (Armstrong), 141

Franciscans, 12, 40-41, 56, 63-64, 82, 121-27; clothing of, 36, 45, 69, 90; forbidden to use horses, 66-67, 70, 109; and problems in order, 58-59, 64-65, 70-71, 121-22, 130; rule of, 65-73; Spiritual, 126, 138; Third Order of, 41, 115, 127, 148. *See also* Lesser Brothers

Francis de Sales, Saint, 40, 87

Francis of Assisi (Frugoni), 143

Francis of Assisi (Moak), 143

Francis of Assisi, Saint
   beliefs and teachings, 41-42, 59, 135, 146; on Christ, 96, 122-23, 131-32, 134-39; on death, 100-102, 111-12; on the gospel, ix-x, 12, 24-26, 28-29, 55, 77, 86, 127-35, 138-39; as orthodox Catholic, ix, 33-35, 41, 52-55, 67, 69, 122, 124, 128-29

   life and death of: family, 4-7, 13-15, 18, 22-23, 25, 113; education, 5-6; as knight, 8, 12, 47, 128; conversion(s), x, 7-8, 11, 13, 19, 25, 132, 144; meeting with Bishop Guido, 14-15, 22, 90, 98, 110-11, 113; meeting with Pope Innocent III, 31-35, 65, 70; clothing, 25, 127-28; as hermit, 40, 46, 127; humility, 21, 98, 113; nakedness, 18-22, 98, 112-13; poverty, 86, 121-22, 128-32, 136; journeys, 37, 46-47, 57, 60-65, 71-72, 109-10, 119, 133; and praise of God, 87-88, 92-95, 99-105; love for creation, 92-95, 98-105, 113, 131, 145; stigmata, 79-91, 108-9, 134, 145; illnesses, 7-8, 40, 109-11; death and burial, 21, 72, 79, 81, 85, 98, 102, 111-14, 116; canonization, 83, 114-17

   work of: with animals, 92-99, 104-5, 114, 131, 137; with lepers, 84, 109, 127, 132; as peacemaker, 96, 102, 119, 124, 133, 136, 146; with the poor, 127, 131-32, 135-36; rebuilding churches, 13-14, 22-24

   writings of, 87-92, 138, 141-42, 148-49; admonitions, 53, 131, 148-49; "Canticle of Brother Sun," 98-103, 110-11, 118, 131; "Canticles of the Creatures," 136; letters, 39, 41, 52-53, 59,

64, 104, 112; prayers, 88-91,
146-49; Rule for Hermitages,
72-73; Rule of 1221 (unsealed
rule), 66-70, 132; Rule of 1223
(sealed rule), 68-71; *Testa-
ment*, 5, 9, 30, 58-59, 68, 91, 121
*Francis of Assisi and His Conver-
sions* (Brunette), 144
*Francis of Assisi: A Revolutionary
Life* (House), 144
Francis of Assisi: Early Documents
(Armstrong, Hellman, and
Short), xi, 141
Francis of Assisi: Index (Armstrong,
Hellman, and Short), 141
Francis of Assisi: The Founder
(Armstrong, Hellman, and
Short), 141
Francis of Assisi: The Prophet
(Armstrong, Hellman, and
Short), 141
Francis of Assisi: The Saint
(Armstrong, Hellman, and
Short), 141
*Franz von Assisi und die Anfange
der Kunst in Italien* (Thode), 106
Frugoni, Chiara, 84, 143

Galatians, Epistle to the, 85
Gandhi, Mohandas, 130, 136
Gargano, Monte, 37
Genesis, Book of, 94, 97, 102-3
Gerasimus, Saint, 98
Germany, Lesser Brothers in, 57
Giles, Brother, 30, 57
Giotto, 14-15, 18, 107, 116-17
Giovanni (noble of Greccio), 74-75

God: and creation, 94-95, 97, 102,
105, 113, 137; grace of, 111; love of,
24, 131; praise of, 87-88, 94-95,
101-5
*God's Fool: The Life and Times of
Saint Francis of Assisi* (Green),
143
Goethe, Johann Wolfgang von, 2,
135
Goorbergh, Edith van den, 141
gospel life, 12, 24, 26, 34, 52, 120-21,
126-28, 138-39
*Gospel Living: Francis of Assisi Yes-
terday and Today* (Rotzetter, Van
Dijk, and Matura), 145
Gospel of Thomas, 22
Gramsci, Antonio, 7
Greccio, 73-77, 86, 91, 95, 106
Green, Julien, 143
Gregorian reform, 123
Gregory VII, ix, 44, 48, 51
Gregory IX, 82, 114-17
grey friars (Franciscans), 36
Greyfriars Review, 140
Grünewald, Matthias, 11
Gualbert, John, 24
Gubbio, 92, 95
Guido, Bishop, 14-15, 22, 90, 98,
110-11, 113

Hardt, Michael, 137
Hellmann, Wayne, 141
Henri of Avanches, 98
Hermitages, Rule for, 72-73
hermits, 23-24, 45; Franciscans as,
72-73, 126. *See also under* Francis
of Assisi, Saint: life and death of

Index

Hippo, bishop of, 123

Hirsau reform (Germany), 27

Historia Occidentalis (de Vitry), 45, 62

History of the Franciscan Order, A (Moorman), 144

Holl, Adolph, 143

Holy Communion. *See* eucharist

Holy Sepulchre, church of the, 64

Holy Thursday, 90, 114

Honorius III, 56, 66, 68, 73, 114-15

Hopkins, Gerard Manley, 79

horses, use of forbidden to Franciscans, 66-67, 70, 109

House, Adrian, 18, 144

Hugh of Saint Victor, 26

Humiliati, 28, 31, 55

humility, 42; of Anthony of Padua, 60; of Christ, 42, 53, 74, 77, 131; of Francis, 21, 98, 113

Ignatius of Loyola, Saint, 7, 77

Illuminato, Brother, 61

Innocent III, 5, 8, 28, 31-35, 47, 50, 56, 90, 114-15

Isaiah, 11, 96, 98

Isenheim altarpiece, 11

Italian Renaissance, vii, ix

Italo-Byzantine art, 105-7; and crucifixes, 13, 85

Italy: art of, 105-7; Francis in, 57, 71-72, 110; places of Franciscan retreat in, 73; provincial synods in, 49

Jacoba of Settesoli, 112-13, 116

Jacopone of Todi, 74, 125-26

Jerome, Saint, 11, 20, 113, 133

Jesus. *See* Christ

Jørgensen, Johannes, vii, 142-43

John, Gospel of, 95, 113-14, 129

John of Saint Paul, 33-34

John of the Cross, Saint, 40, 108, 113

John Paul II, 1, 118, 136

John the Baptist, 19-20

Joseph (father of Jesus), 74

Kazantzakis, Nikos, viii, 142-43

LaChance, Paul, 25

La Croix, 147

Lady Poverty, 2, 21, 89, 128

Lapsanski, Duane, 28

La Rocca Maggiore, 3-4

Last Christian, The (Holl), 143

Lateran Councils, 47-52, 122, 124, 127; First (1123), 49; Second (1139), 28, 49; Third (1179), 10, 49; Fourth (1215), ix, 32, 42, 47-52, 54-58, 67, 90, 122

La Verna, Mount, viii, 13, 45, 77-79, 81-82, 85-87, 108

Lazarus (Luke 16), 10

Legenda Major (Bonaventure), 15, 18, 34, 75, 82, 90, 95, 109, 112, 114, 122

Legend of the Three Companions, 36

Leo, Brother, 82, 87-89, 116

Leo, Count, 46

Leonard of Saint Maurice, 91

lepers, 9-13, 27; and Francis, 9, 11-

12, 22-25, 127, 132; and Jesus, 10-11

Lesser Brothers, 43-45, 58-60. *See also* Franciscans

letters: from Clare, 39; from Elias of Cortona, 79, 81, 84, 114; from Francis, 39, 41, 52-53, 59, 64, 104, 112

Leviticus, purity codes of, 10

liberation theology, 132, 143

Liege, 43

Life of Saint Antony (Athanasius), 23

Life of Saint Francis of Assisi, (Sabatier), vii, 121, 138, 142

Little Flowers of Saint Francis, 96

Little Portion. *See* Portiuncula

Lives of the Saints (Butler), vii

Lombardy, 28

Lord's Prayer, 88

Lorenzetti, Pietro, 116

Louise de Marillac, Saint, 40

love: of God, 26, 131; of neighbor, 26, 42

Luther, Martin, 123, 126

Lyons, 27, 31

Major Life. See Legenda Major

Malik-al-Kamil, 61-63, 119, 133

Manselli, Raoul, 143

Marches of Italy, 72, 109

Mark the Hermit, Saint, 97

Marquis de la Rochetulon, 147

marriage: arranged, 27; prohibited, 37, 45, 49

Martha (and Mary), 72

Martin, Valerie, 144

Martini, Simone, 116

Martin of Tours, Saint, 12, 116

martyrdom, 37, 47, 59

Marx, Karl, 137

Mary (and Martha), 72

Mary (mother of Jesus), 74, 86, 88, 101

Masseo, Brother, 116

Master of the Saint Francis Cycle, 14-15, 18, 117

Matura, Thaddeus, 145

Maurin, Peter, 40, 136

McGinn, Bernard, 135, 145

mercantilism, 3-4, 127, 129, 138

Messiaen, Olivier, 137

Middle East, 57, 63, 65

Milan, 27

militancy, 137-38

Minerva, temple of, 2, 15

Mirror of Perfection, 12

Misadventure of Francis of Assisi, The: Towards a Historical Use of the Franciscan Legends (Dalarun), 144

Moak, Helen, 143

Mohammad, 47

monastic tradition, 19, 26-27, 32, 44-45, 56, 73, 123, 128-29

Monte Casale, 109

Moorman, John, 144

Morocco, 46, 59, 63

Mother Earth, 102, 113

music, and Christian life, 139

Muslim lands, journeys to, 37, 46-47, 57, 59-60, 63-64, 124

Mussolini, Benito, 138

nakedness: of Adam, 20-21, 97, 113; of Christ, 20, 74, 98, 113; of Francis, 18-22, 98, 112-13
nativity, dramatization of, 75-77, 91, 106
Negri, Antonio, 137-38
Nicholas III, 83
Nicholas IV, 117
nudity. *See* nakedness
Numbers, Book of, 88

Ockham, William of, 125
Offreduccio family, 5, 37. *See also* Clare, Saint
Olivi, Peter John, 125
Origins of the Franciscan Order, The (Esser), 144
Orwell, George, 120
Osservatore Romano, 147-48
Ozanam, Frederic, vii

Padua, 60
Palm Sunday, 37-38, 46
Paradiso (Dante), 21, 57, 107
Paris, University of, 115, 125-26
Passover, feast of, 114
Patarines of Milan, 27, 129
Paul, Saint, 18-20, 83-86
Paul VI, 48
penance: Francis as man of, 9, 25, 37, 52, 126; and Franciscans, 33-34, 53, 69, 90; fruits of, 42; men of, 9, 22-23, 112; as preached by Francis, 53-54, 71
Pentecost chapter of 1217, 56-59, 65
Perugia, 2, 5, 7, 56, 114
Pescia altarpiece, 93-94, 134

Peter (associate of Francis), 30
Peterson, Ingrid, 37, 142
Philip (associate of Francis), 30
Philippians, Epistle to the, 20
Pilate, 131
pilgrimage: to Assisi, 61-62, 73, 117-18, 133; to Jerusalem, 63-64, 91; to Padua, 60; to Rome, 37
Pio, Padre, 83
Pius XI, 83
Pius XII, 60
Poetes Franciscans, Les (Ozanam), vii
Poor Clares (Poor Ladies), 39-40, 100-102, 115, 126
Poor Men of Lyons. *See* Waldensians
popes: authority of, 32, 52; elections of, 49; and Francis, 31-35, 65, 70, 132; and Franciscans, 38, 47, 65-66, 121-22, 124, 126
Portiuncula (chapel), 23, 30, 35, 37, 56-57, 59, 108, 111-12, 118, 136
possessions, lack of, 18, 25-26, 36, 66, 69, 77, 129, 131
poverty, 23, 26-27; of Christ, 25, 27, 30, 39, 42, 54, 74, 77, 85, 124, 129-32; of Clare, 37-41; as Franciscan ideal, 18, 21-22, 33-34, 38-41, 52, 74, 85, 121-26, 129-32, 136; privilege of, 38
Poverty and Joy: The Franciscan Tradition (Short), 145
"Praise of the Virtues" (Francis), 149
"Praises of God" (Francis), 87-88

Prayer of Saint Francis, The (Boff), 148

Preachers, Order of. *See* Dominicans

preaching: of Dominicans, 56-57; of Franciscans, 30, 34-35, 43, 67, 69-70, 111, 124, 130, 135; itinerant, 25-27, 31; lay, 25, 31, 34; license to, 28

Premontre, 27

priesthood, 42, 51, 52, 54, 58

Psalms, 87-88, 90-94, 102-3, 114

Radical Reformation, 126

Reformation, 48, 135

reform of the church, 26-27, 32, 44, 51, 54, 71, 115, 122-24, 128. *See also* Lateran Councils

Regula Bullata (sealed rule), 68-71, 73, 115

regula non-bullata (unsealed rule), 33, 66-70

religio, Franciscan order as, 35-36, 71, 115, 121-22, 127

Reluctant Saint: The Life of Francis of Assisi (Spoto), 144

Renaissance, 107, 121; art of, 106

Renan, Joseph-Ernest, 121

Respectfully Yours: Signed and Sealed Francis of Assisi (Goorbergh and Zweerman), 141

Rieti, 68

Robert of Abrissel, 26

Robert of Xanten, Saint, 27

Robson, Michael, 143

Roman calendar, 84

Romans, Epistle to the, 19, 95

romanticism, 135, 138

Rome: Francis in, 32, 46-47, 50; Lateran councils in, 48-50, 55; pilgrimage to, 37

Rotzetter, Anton, 145

Rufino, Brother, 116

Rule (Benedict), 24

Rule (Clare), 39-40

Rule of 1221. *See regula non-bullata*

Rule of 1223. *See Regula Bullata*

Sabatier, Paul, vii, 54, 121-22, 138, 142

Sacro Specchio, 134

Sacrum Commercium, 21

Saint Francis (Boff), 143

Saint Francis of Assisi (Englebert), 143

Saint Francis of Assisi (Manselli), 143

Saint Francis of Assisi: A Biography (Jørgensen), 142

St. Francis of Assisi and Nature (Sorrell), 145

Saint Francis of Assisi: Omnibus of Sources, 141

Saint Francis of Assisi: The Legend and the Life (Robson), 143

Saint Francis of Assisi: Writings for a Gospel Life (Armstrong), 141

Saint Francois d'Assise (Messiaen), 137

"Saint of Authority and Saint of the Spirit" (Talar), 142

Salvation: Scenes from the Life of St. Francis (Martin), 144

Sanctity and Secularity during the

Index

Modernist Period: Six Perspectives on Hagiography circa 1900 (Barmann and Talar, eds.), 142

San Damiano: church of, 13-14, 22, 38, 39, 40, 100, 117; convent of, 109-10, 112, 118

San Giorgio, church of, 114, 116-17

San Pietro, church of, 23

San Rufino, cathedral of, 3-4, 118

Santa Croce, church of, 15, 107

Santa Maria Novella, 107

Saracens, 61, 67, 69

"Sayings of Light and Love" (John of the Cross), 113

Schmucki, Octavian, 145

Segni, 114-15

seraph, Francis's vision of, 81-82, 84, 87

Sextus Propertius, 2

Shi'ite mystics, 85

Short, William, 141, 145

skete (Orthodox monastic settlement), 73

"Song of Roland, The," 46

Sorrell, Roger, 145

Soul's Journey to God, The (Bonaventure), 86-87, 94-95

Souvenir Normand, 147-48

Spain, 46

Spiritual Exercises (Ignatius of Loyola), 77

Spiritual Franciscans: From Protest to Persecution in the Century after Saint Francis (Burr), 144

Spoto, Donald, 144

Stefano, friar, 64

stigmata, 82-87; of Francis, 80-91, 108-9, 134, 145

Stigmata of St. Francis, The (Schmucki), 145

Subasio, Monte, 1, 31, 73, 117

Sufi brotherhood, 62

Sylvester (priest of Assisi), 30-31

Syria, 57, 60

Talar, C. J., 142

TAU, mark of the, 86, 89-90

Tennyson, Alfred Lord, 95

Teresa of Avila, Saint, 40, 47, 87

Testament (Francis), 5, 9, 30, 58-59, 68, 91, 121

Thode, Henry, 106

Thomas Aquinas, Saint, 8, 57, 94

Thomas of Celano, 4, 6, 19, 21, 25, 73-76, 81-82, 84, 90, 94, 104-5, 134

tithes, 36

transubstantiation, 51

Tunis, 57

Ugolino (Hugolin), Cardinal, 57, 115

Urban II, 27

Van Dijk, Willibrod-Christian, 145

Venice, 64

Vincent de Paul, Saint, 40

Virtuoso Theology (Young), 139

vita evangelica. See gospel life

Vitalis of Savigny, 27

Vitry, Jacques de, 43-46, 56, 62

Voltaire, 135

Vulgate translation of the Bible, 11

Index

Waldensians (Poor Men of Lyons),
28, 31, 34, 42, 50, 55, 129
Waldo, Peter, 27-28
Walter of Brienne, 8
Weber, Max, 122
Weil, Simone, 118, 136
wolf of Gubbio, 92, 95
wolves, and Francis, 95-96
Word: Christ as, 42, 53, 102; and
creation, 105; as flesh, 74, 85, 105,
129; of God, 54-55, 95, 139
"Wreck of the Deutschland, The"
(Hopkins), 79

Young, Frances, 139

Zeferelli, Franco, viii
Zweerman, Theodore, 141